dispatches from hell

*a vegan's guide to love, sex, relationships
and other suicidal tendencies*

by daniel peyser

tofu hound press

First Printing 2006

Tofu Hound Press
PO Box 276
Colton, NY 13625
publications@tofuhound.com

SAN: 256-7091

Sign up for updates from the publisher and explore our other titles at http://tofuhound.com

Contact the author c/o Tofu Hound Press or via the website for this book at: http://dispatchesfromhell.org

ISBN-10: 0-9770804-0-4
ISBN-13: 978-0-9770804-0-3

Cover/Interior design and production by Fourteen Little Men, Inc.
www.fourteenlittlemen.com

To Jenna,
This would have been a
very different book
without you.

To my parents,
You taught me everything
I know about relationships, except the
sex stuff. Also, I hope you will never read this.

To Team Torres,
For making the dream come true.
You're the wind beneath my wings….
or do I mean 'anus?'

~~To My Exes,~~

table of contents

Introduction

If you're reading this, chances are it's because you're not only single, but vegan as well. If you're reading this, it's probably because you're tired of feeling like you're one at the expense of the other. If you're reading this, it's because you need some answers. Unfortunately I don't have any, because if you're reading this, it's because you're just like me. However, in the pages that follow, perhaps we can hash out some issues and address some tough questions all vegan singles wrestle with—most important of all, what exactly does it mean to be vegan and single in a world of omnivores? I can't promise easy answers, and if I did, then I'd think less of you for reading this book; there are no easy answers, and anyone who tells you otherwise is either full of shit, or full of themselves. And while I may be full of shit, I am generally not known for being full of myself. What I can offer is some insight and companionship, if only on paper, in what is frequently a lonesome and frightening journey. It may not be everything you're looking for and more, but I can assure you it's probably better than what you've already got.

As any vegan knows, being vegan lands you in some weird spots. Then again, as any vegan of a couple of years or more knows, the fact that you're vegan also becomes second nature, something you don't necessarily think about all that much on a day-to-day basis, aside from the typical bullshit flak you catch from the world of omnis. However, the one time you are guaranteed to not only notice, but be hyperaware you're vegan, is when it comes to being single, or more aptly, trying actively to alleviate your singleness. Omnis always ask us, "Is it hard being vegan?" and the answer is always "No" (or at least it should be, unless you're a whiny bitch). But there's one glaring exception, isn't there? In the already awkward, terrifying, and demoralizing world of dating, your veganism catapults from being just another part of who you are to a matter of great consequence. Suddenly, it's something you *are* thinking about—you're thinking about it a lot, because it erects an entirely new and seemingly insurmountable barrier of awkwardness, terror, and demoralization to something most omnis already seem to have a hard enough time getting right. We'll try to tackle this veritable Everest of difficulties together. But before we begin our journey of love, growth, and unyielding trauma, there are some things you should know up front.

This book is written from a male's perspective. You might as well find out sooner rather than later. That having been said, I think most of this stuff probably goes both ways; or perhaps it's just that I hope it does. I can't speak for all vegan women, and I definitely can't speak for all vegan guys. But, invariably, as with every other area of a vegan life, there are going to be some commonalities—quite a few, I imagine.

Oh, and one last thing: I'm not what most people call "politically correct." While this isn't something I'm particularly ashamed of, it's one last thing I should be up-front about so there are no unpleasant surprises for you, dear reader, somewhere farther down the bravely-trodden road of vegan singles, dating, and relationships. I will refer to men as "guys," women as "chicks," and the words "dick," "cunt," "twat," "asshole," "bitch," and "douchebag" are all likely to crop up. I make no apologies, but I figure you should still have a chance to get your money back before reading any more if this sort of thing will sincerely offend you. Also, if you're uptight about sex, you bought the wrong book. Or maybe you bought the right book—a book that will help bring you out of your prudish shell. But more likely you bought the wrong book, because there's a whole, big chapter on sex, and it's pretty explicit, if I do say so myself (which I do).

And now, without further ado, the book.

chapter 1

Vegan & Single

Some people really do enjoy being single. I, unfortunately or otherwise, am not one of them. Some people view it as "freedom"—I view it as the freedom to be bored and lonely. For me, and probably you, being single sucks some serious ass. One of the best things in life, whether or not we give it much thought, is being vegan. Sadly, one of the worst things in life is being vegan and single. It's a tough situation to remedy, and it's easy to get down on yourself. My first piece of advice? Don't. Don't get down on yourself. Somewhere out there is another vegan just like you. You may never meet them, and you probably won't end up spending the rest of your life with them, but it can still be comforting to know you're not really as alone as you think.

Being vegan and single leaves you with only a handful of options. One, for those of you who have made the great leap into the digital age, is online dating. In my limited experience, most people tend to stray from and/or look down on online dating. It's hard to feel like you've been reduced to the point where it seems the internet is your last chance to find true love. The upshot to online dating or singles sites is that you can specify you want someone vegan. The downside is having to live with the fact that you had to try to use the internet, rather than your own questionably good looks and vegan charm to find another soul like you. That, and having to explain to your friends, "This is my new girlfriend. We met online!"

Then there's the bar scene. Most people wouldn't think it, but a lot of us vegans like to party, and some of us do it particularly hard and on a regular basis. Going out clubbing or to bars can be a great way to meet other people. However, it can also be a great recipe for making you feel even more alone than you already do, being faced with an endless sea of cuties, hotties, and everything in between, forced to acknowledge the fact that they are not for you. Why? Because you can pretty much guarantee yourself not a single one of them is vegan. Also, you have to consider the sort of person that goes out to bars all the time. You might go because you're somewhat desperate, and hopeful that your lucky night will finally come when you meet that other stray vegan. You have to remember though, that omnis don't have that problem. Consequently, many of the kind folks you'll meet out at the bars and clubs aren't looking for what I'm told Facebook[1] users refer to as an "LTR," that is, a long-term relationship.

Another option is social events. If you're vegan, you probably have some inkling of interest in matters of social justice. And if you're not already involved in some sort of local group along these lines, attending events and getting involved can be a good way to meet potential partners as well as do something meaningful. Of course, if you have a local animal rights group, then you're probably set and may not even need to read this book. But thanks in advance if you do anyway. The downside for me is that many of these groups consist of what I like to call "hippy-ass liberals." I don't say this as a conservative of some sort, because I'm a Marxist. What I mean is, these groups frequently consist of protest tourists involved in the cause *du jour*. But, if you're lucky, maybe you run into a really cool radical vegan chick.

The final and perhaps most common option is to just stay home, or go about your daily business and hope an intelligent, cute, vegan counterpart will simply fall from the sky in some moment of ultimate

---

1 For those of you unfamiliar with Facebook, it's a way people build an online persona to keep in touch with friends they could just as easily ring on the phone. Mostly used by borderline-stalker personalities.

10

serendipity. Hopefully we all see the downsides to this approach without me needing to go into detail.

As you can see, we vegan singles don't have a whole lot of options.

Well, wait. There is one last option. You could just date a non-vegan. At least, this is what my friends tell me. I know this seems in many ways like the most tempting option. After all, you could have it just as easy as the omnis when it comes to relationships, couldn't you? I mean after all, you deserve it. Why should they have it so easy? When they go to restaurants they get to *pick* between dishes. When they go clothes shopping, they can go pretty much anywhere and wear pretty much anything. Us? We have to look for the animal product alternatives, frequently more expensive than "the real thing." So why do they get to have all the fun when it comes to relationships? It might be just as easy to slip undercover into the omni dating scene. Let me tell *you* just why I think that's a really, really bad idea if you haven't figured it out for yourself yet. The truth is, while in many areas of life omnis and vegans aren't all that different, when it comes to relationships we are worlds apart. Allow me to explicate.

I've been vegan for a pretty damn long while (at the time of this writing, a little over seven years). It's not something I ever think about on a day-to-day basis any longer, except when I'm blogging or trying to have a peaceful meal in my current or previous omni workplaces. On the whole, however, my being vegan is almost never an issue anymore. Except when it comes to dating—then, suddenly, it's a *big fucking issue*.

Take this scenario: on any given night you'll find me in one bar or another. Of course I have my favorite, but I like to circulate as well. Truth be told—as I mentioned above—bars are not exactly the greatest place to meet prospective dates, but there's something about a woman who likes her whiskey that I find totally irresistible. Chances that this woman will be vegan? Let's put it this way: there's probably a better chance she's been struck by lightning, won the lottery, *and* met the pope (which pope? I'll leave that up to you, sweet reader).

Why does it matter whether or not she's vegan?

This is a question my omni friends always ask. While I don't have the most amazing luck with women—to which the majority of friends, and my own mother, could attest—I've been around enough to learn a few things about dating non-vegans, both vegetarian and omni, as well as the downsides to dating ready-made vegans.

Things I've Learned About Dating:

Omni chicks just don't get it. Omni girls don't get the vegan thing. You become an oddity at worst, and fetishized at best for your veganism. Worse yet is meeting omnis who "used to be" veg*n. They are just fucking obnoxious.

Omni women smell bad. Yes, up top and down below, omni women are, shall we say, "unpleasant" in the fragrance department. I never used to believe this until dating a few omni girls, and nearly across the board I found this to be the case. I know it sounds bad, but what the fuck, it's the truth. It's probably a trite point, but if you're vegan and you've dated omnis, you probably know this to be true as well. Omni chicks are totally fucking treyf.

Vegetarian women can be converted. I don't actively recruit for the Church of Veganism, and especially not in relationships. But I have dated a couple of veggie girls for a while, both of whom eventually just became vegan over the course of the respective relationships. So this isn't a bad thing, then, just something I've learned. There is one bad downside though—*most veggies dislike/hate/feel uncomfortable around vegans.* That's because veggies subconsciously feel like they're half-assing it or being judged when they are around vegans, and that's why they are often more hostile to us than even the most meat-loving omni. At least, that's how I rationalize their often-juvenile bullshit to which I am frequently subjected.

Many vegans are hippies, trustafarians,[2] *or some other sort of ass-chapping personality type.* I hate jam bands. I especially hate Phish (this matters even more, as I'm a Vermonter). With scant exceptions, dreads are not meant for white people (I say this as an ex-dreadhead). Bob Marley is okay as background music at the Caribbean restaurant, but I can't really listen to much music that glorifies psychotic emperors like Haile Selassie. I don't have a Ben & Jerry's bumper sticker that reads, "If it's not fun, why do it?" I am not really that into Foucault, patchouli, cocaine, white water rafting, hiking and camping, pacifism, Zion or Zionism, the Green Party, Gandhi, knitting circles, yoga, realigning my chakras, going to that sand mandala showing downtown, or freeing Tibet (i.e., I'm not quite that "down" with feudal theocracies). Sorry.

Even if you meet a vegan, there's no guarantee things will work out, or that they will even like you at all. Most of my omni friends worry they'll never meet that special someone. On the off chance I even *meet* another vegan—and you'd think where I live, in Burlington, Vermont, it wouldn't be that hard, but it is—there is an excellent chance things will not work out anyway. That's because things like personality, looks, and all the other characteristics omnis possess still come into play right after someone passes the V-test. This is perhaps the ultimately shitty part of being vegan and single: knowing that even if by some stretch of the imagination you meet some other vegan cutie, they may not even like you. And even if they do, there's an even better chance things will just not work out. Go ahead and call me pessimistic. Then again, I'd rather be pleasantly surprised when my pessimism (I call it "pragmatism," but whatever) is proven wrong, than be an optimist and be taken off guard by constant disappointment.

Okay, I know I said not to get down on yourself, and it sounds like that's what I'm doing here. And maybe I am. Just a little. But in general, I try to stay positive. Regardless, these are the reasons I think trying to join the dating world of the omnis is a rather fruitless exercise in

---

2   This denotes any trust fund baby with dreadlocks who likes Phish, the Dead, Bob Marley, or thinks they are, in fact, Jamaican. Notable for their frequent references to "Jah Rastafari," or having dogs named "Irie."

absurdity, and why even if you bump into the stray vegan out there in the omni bars, it's not necessarily anything to be optimistic about. Sometimes that can be an even bigger let-down than not meeting any. What's worse? Wondering if they're out there and never meeting them, or *knowing* they're out there but it ain't gonna happen?

Confession Time, dear reader: after giving you all the reasons not to date an omni, I'm going to complicate things a little and totally contradict myself. Everything I said about the subject up until this very sentence? It's true. Well, mostly. Dating omnis isn't a totally bad idea, and here's why: if you're like me, you don't have a very large PVDP (that's Potential Vegan Dating Pool in my personal lexicon). Refusing to date omnis may end up meaning you just never date. Period. This doesn't mean you have to compromise, though. Here's the deal, or at least what I've found to be true: if someone is enough like you that you could see yourself with them for a very long time, it's likely because you share the same basic values in life. Chances are, the same values that led you to veganism are values the omni in question possesses—they just haven't manifested themselves in the form of veganism. Yet. That's where you come in. I'm not saying you should actively try to convert them. But if they are as into you as you are to them, they will want to understand you in a deeper way, and that means understanding why you are vegan. When confronted with your reasons for going vegan, there is a pretty good chance they will go vegan as well.

Here's where I open all up

I met Jenna (at the time not vegan) when I was in college. She was in a student activist group with me. At the time, I was involved with somewhat long-distance relationship with another girl (at the time vegan). Jenna and I were close friends, but nothing more. After college, while debating the option of grad school, I moved to Montana with the vegan girl, who was still an undergrad and transferring to the U of M from a school in Boston. We had been together for a couple of years, and by about half way through the third, it became abundantly clear the relationship had, to put it lightly, gone to shit. I packed my things and came home with my tail between my legs.

After settling into an apartment with an old best friend from high school and two other guys, I tried to get back on my feet in the relationship arena. Things weren't so hot. I tried bars, clubs, and even dated a girl for a while who was vegan (although she did cheat from time to time; on veganism, that is, not me... at least as far as I know). After a couple of months, that relationship didn't work out either. I was more than a bit distraught. What was I doing wrong?

It was around this time Jenna had returned from a year studying in Spain. We agreed it had been too long, and that we'd meet up. After a few phone calls and failed attempts, and one flat tire, Jenna finally made it to Burlington. From the moment she pulled up in her car in front of my driveway, it was obvious something was different, something had changed, although I couldn't tell if it was her, me, or both of us. Regardless, it was wonderful to see her. We went out for drinks that night. As Jenna was still an omni, I wasn't exactly thinking of her in romantic terms. By morning, that had all changed for both of us.[3]

It wasn't until later, when we were having dinner with my mom that weekend, that reality set in. I was having portabella mushroom, they were having chicken. As fork after fork of grilled flesh found its way into her mouth, it dawned on me that this might be an issue. After dinner, I stopped thinking about it. And, as days passed, Jenna became more interested in why exactly I was vegan. She had always known I was vegan, and consequently it meant a lot to me. The rest? Well, I'll let her tell that part.

When I reconnected with Dan, I was probably more of an omni than I had ever been in my life. I'd just returned from ten months living with a host family in Madrid. While I was there, my basic food groups were reduced to two: meat and eggs. My host family put them on my plate at every meal. I also developed a rather serious addiction

---

3   No, we didn't have tons of sex. We'll get to this later in the dating chapter.

to the Spanish café con leche (strong coffee with lots of milk). What's worse, I had fallen into a deep moral ambivalence about a great many things. I willingly traded all my money for whisky at the bars three or four (or five) nights a week. I smoked a lot, and not just cigarettes, mind you. I couldn't hold down a relationship to save my life. I didn't do shit in terms of any kind of activism or community work. In other words, I was a shamefully self-indulgent, carnivorous, apolitical bum. And a lush. And deeply unhappy. Of course, coming back to the states just exacerbated the situation.

But then, about a month after I got back to the US, as I was sinking deeper and deeper into depression and hopelessness about the state of things, I went to visit Dan. That's when everything changed. I saw Dan again after so much time, and he jolted me out of my apathetic existence, and out of my depression as well. You see, one of the things that I have always loved about Dan is his ability to commit to the things that are important to him. He has always been committed to Marxism, to veganism and animal rights, to actively opposing exploitation and oppression of human and non-human animals, and to his friends. And he is committed not just in word, like most people, but in action. Of course, when I had hung out with him before, he was also always committed to a certain aforementioned ex-girlfriend, which placed him outside any realm of possible romantic interests. Not so now. We hit it off, fell in love, and it was the easiest thing in the world to make a commitment to him. Hell, it was the only natural thing to do. It is the only thing I have been sure about in my life. But what of veganism in all this?

The first couple days we were together, I was too crazy in love to think too much about becoming vegan. Dan and I share a great deal of political and moral views, we both smoke lots of cigarettes, we both love a good whisky, we're goofy, we're honest with each other, we make each other laugh, we're both hopelessly nerdy. So the fact that he was a vegan and I was an omni seemed like a rather insignificant difference in the scheme of things at first. I ate mostly vegan when I was with him, but continued to put cream in my coffee without a second thought, and *when Dan's mom offered me chicken, I ate it with little remorse. After a few days though, I started realizing that Dan's veganism was a really important part of who he is. It finally dawned on me that whether I became vegan or not, I had the responsibility to learn as much as I could about the subject. It is such a significant and meaningful part of who he is. If I was to really love all of who he is, I would have to understand every last bit of him. So I began asking all the common asinine questions that omnis ask vegans.*

Dan was the perfect vegan mentor, of course. He patiently answered all my stupid questions, and put up with me bitching and moaning about how hard it would be to give up wool, honey, cheese, ice cream, etc. He never pressured me to become vegan, he never preached, he never made me feel guilty. He recommend books and websites to check out, and he explained why he is vegan. From what Dan told me, it became increasingly clear to me that there was absolutely no logical or ethical argument against veganism. And so began the battle in my head—the battle between the logical, rational and compassionate on the one side, and the whiny, tradition-bound, self-indulgent part of me on the other. Once I saw it in those terms, the choice was pretty clear.

Nevertheless, it seemed to me that if I wanted to become vegan and stay vegan, that I would have to do it on my own terms. It wasn't something that I could do for Dan, it was something that I had to want to do for myself. So I neglected all other responsibilities, and sifted through zillions of websites on ethical veganism for the better part of two days. By the end of my vegan literature binge, I had decided that I definitely wanted to become vegan, but I also started thinking of all the things that I couldn't possibly give up. I made all sorts of plans to wean myself off animal products. I was vegetarian for a couple days, and that was easy. I kept talking to Dan about it, and he offered continued support and encouragement, but never pressure. Finally, I read Vegan Freak: Being Vegan in a Non-Vegan World *by Bob and Jenna Torres, and before I was through the second chapter, I decided to use their cold-tofu approach and quit animal products altogether that very moment. The combination of their personal experiences going vegan and the connections that they laid out between animal exploitation and other systems of exploitation under capitalism pushed me into the land of vegan freakdom, and I haven't looked back.*

I've been vegan for only about five months at the time of this writing, but I can say that it was far easier than I ever imagined it could be. I am certain I will never go back. The hardest part was getting past that initial mental block, and the first couple weeks of painstakingly slow label reading of everything, and from there on out it has been cake. Dan and I gorge ourselves on delicious vegan food together all the time, and I hardly think about the fact that I am vegan, unless I have to deal with shit from omnis or vegetarians. Beyond all that, though, I think our mutual commitment to veganism has strengthened our love and commitment to each other, and vice versa. Our love for each other has made us all the more compassionate towards the other life around us. Vegan relationships really are absolute fucking bliss. But enough with the boring cheesy stuff, I'll pass you back to Dan. He's far more entertaining than I am.[4]

So you see, the fact that someone's an omni is not an immediate barrier to a relationship with them, nor is it a barrier to them becoming vegan. If, however, it becomes clear the omni in question will never become vegan, you're going to have to decide your own limits. What if the relationship gets more serious? Can you deal with the fact they aren't vegan? Here's where many vegans, myself included, would say no. If you've been with your partner for awhile now and they still haven't at least begun the move towards a more vegan lifestyle, then chances are that move isn't going to happen anytime soon, if ever. And really, if it comes to this, it's likely because they don't necessarily share those core values you thought they might, which, veganism aside, could be a big red flag for other problems to crop up somewhere down the line. But perhaps we're getting ahead of ourselves. Let's start with the basics.

---

4   Author's note: this is, in point of fact, entirely questionable.

Here's where I'm done opening all up

Being single is important. If you're one of those people (and here I mean, "If you're like me,") who is constantly in relationships, it is even harder to be single for any amount of time, but that makes it even more important to be. It's not wrong to define yourself with or against someone else, but if your relationships keep failing as you skip from one to the next, a big part of the problem is likely that you can't define who you are without the context of someone else. This isn't good.

There are few things I hate more than when people have dumped me citing the need to "get to know themselves." Normally, that actually meant "sleep with your friends." But for you, the better, nicer, non-ex-of-mine, it is critical for you to have some time to yourself. You have to know what you want, what you like, what you're into, all that stuff. It's not just important for you, either. It's necessary to have the time to do this if you hope to ever not be single for more than a few months per relationship. That's because it's these very things—what you want, like, are into—that make you interesting, that make someone else want to be with you. If your desires are constantly expressed in terms of theirs, you aren't very interesting, nor is it very healthy for you to be in such a situation. Oh, and they'll cheat on you with someone with "more to offer." I'm not saying it's a bad thing if you and your partner's likes, dislikes, desires, and interests are the same, just that it's a bad thing if they aren't genuinely yours when you aren't with anyone else. The key to being happy with anyone else is being happy with yourself first.

This makes me particularly unqualified to give you any advice, as I've rarely been happy with myself. There's no easy recipe, but you do need to learn to value yourself. Not in an egotistical, preening sense; just that you don't contemplate different ways to end your life when you wake up every morning.

Owning your shitty singleness

There are ways to ease the pain, annoyance, and boredom of single life. Once you can master them, then we're ready to move on to the dating chapter.

Friends. Friends are important. Even if you're a total loner like me, you should have at least one or two. Preferably two, because sometimes one fucks you over, and if that was the only one you had, you're kind of shit-out-of-luck, aren't you? If you don't really have any friends, try meeting them at functions that involve stuff you like to do. Even if you're a total loser, I promise there are other people who like the stuff you do, whether it's anime, rock collecting, *D&D*, or midget bukkake. What you do with your friends is up to you. But they will provide you with the support you'll need later in life, as well as boost your self-esteem a bit.

Hands. Oh, you'll need these too. Missing both your hands? Well, I hope your feet are flexible. Because you're going to have to "satisfy" yourself. Jerking off gets a bad name. Here's what I mean: each girl who masturbates thinks she's the only one who does it, or at least close to the only one. Trust me, they all do it. It's normal, not unnatural. A lot of them do it just as much as guys. And guys? Well, we do it *a lot*. And that gets to another point: for some reason, people think they jerk off too much. I love seeing letters to love advice columnists that read, "I think I jerk off too much. I do it like three times a day sometimes." Three times a day? To which I say: come on. Is that the best you can do?

Substance abuse. Okay, I don't really think you should become a substance abuser. I'm not even sure why I put that one in there. It doesn't really make being single *easier, per se.* Also, it will probably make you a pretty unappealing potential partner to anyone else.

Exercise. I've never tried this one, but I hear it's great. Exercising releases all sorts of fun endorphins that make you happy. Also, you'll get in better shape. I don't really care much about feeling happy or getting in shape, so I've never exercised much.[5] If you get a gym membership, you may even meet some people that way. Sign up for a spinning class or some such shit. This way, you get to feel better, look better, be healthier, and put yourself out there to meet people. And if you want to meet someone really flexible *and,* failing that, be able to blow yourself,[6] sign up for a yoga class.

Hobbies. These are important to keep you sane. When you're not at work, you'll want to be doing other stuff, whether you like to cook, write, read, draw, paint, play music, watch movies, or whatever. I guess whacking off also constitutes a hobby, as it was certainly one of mine growing up. Some people I know or talk to complain they don't really have anything like this to do, or that "I'm just not good at anything." That's a total load of bullshit. Everyone's good at something. Whatever it is you finally take an interest in, you just have to be patient. It'll come to you.

Once you've managed to get these things right, or some variation of them, you're ready to enter the wide, wild, and less than wonderful world of dating.

---

5   Unless sex counts. And why shouldn't it? I've had a lot of sex. That's totally exercise, and bollocks to anyone who says otherwise.

6   I should say here I'm not sure how enjoyable this would actually be. But I'm not that flexible, and also hate yoga, so I wouldn't really know.

chapter **2**

On The Prowl: The Dating Vegan

You *are* a wonderful person. You *can* realize your goals. You *will* have what you desire. Okay, fuck that, this isn't that kind of book. You might be a wonderful person, you might be able to realize your goals, and you might have what you ultimately desire but probably not—at least on the last two counts—especially when it comes to dating. I've said it before in other venues and, frankly, it's something that bears repeating: dating is for losers. You've got a better shot with the online shit than with dating, and just think of the losers who do that.[1] You're probably wondering, just about now, why I chose to title this chapter "The Dating Vegan" if dating is indeed, as I have suggested, "for losers." Honestly, I just couldn't think of a better word. I tossed around "courtship" for a bit, but ditched it because it seemed to imply you've already set your sights on someone. Also because, as my publishers put it, this book is being published in the *twenty-first* century.

So what to do, if not date? Well, one possibility is that you're already in a relationship. In that case, this chapter might still be fun, but it may not be very helpful. Feel free to skip ahead to the chapter on love. But

---

1   For the record, as research for this book I did register on just about any online dating site possible for vegans. Then again, I've never denied being a loser. In retrospect, this is probably to my credit.

my advice? Actively search. This is different from dating, and probably more frustrating in that the mere act of keeping your eyes peeled 24/7 will make the lack of results even less bearable. But, trust me, dating sucks somethin' fierce, and this way you'll save yourself a nasty bar tab. If you've got to learn this for yourself, so be it. But don't go sending me the bill. I'm still trying to pay off my own. A lot of my friends complain about their college loans. At least they got a degree out of it. Me? Well, let's just say very some lucky children of Pabst factory workers will never need to worry about paying off college loans again, and that's counting inflation.

One useful way to approach the hunt[2] is to think of yourself as a fishing hook (see footnote again, please). You've got to wear some bait, otherwise you're fucked, and not in the good relationship-finding kind of way. I find the easiest way to do this is wear some vegan or animal-rights related t-shirts. These tend to make you less approachable for omnis, thereby driving away flattering, though pointless, bites. Conversely, they attract positive attention from folks who are veg*n.[3] While this isn't categorically true, it definitely helps. You can go with the less offensive, more direct route with shirts that simply say "Vegan," or the potentially more offensive, more explicit route with shirts like "Vegans taste better," or "Beef: It's what's rotting in your colon." Bait like this will help draw any vegans out of the crowd.

Remember how I said dating was for losers a couple of paragraphs ago? Well, it kind of is. Kind of. You'll still want to go out with the person you meet, and as that's technically considered a "date," that's how I'll be referring to it for the rest of the chapter. Don't get me wrong, asking every girl you meet at the bar out on dates is for losers and will fail miserably, much like all of your past "dating" efforts (I'm going to make an assumption here that they did fail, which I'd imagine to be the case if you're reading this).

---

2   Yeah, I know, not exactly the most vegan term. Whatever. Bite me.

3   Vegetarian or vegan.

Vegan Dating (Or, Now that We've Established Dating Sucks and is Totally, Totally Lame)

Dating for vegans can be surprisingly easy, as most restaurants will only have one or two menu options for you anyway. Of course, that assumes you've got a date. But before you decide on the most veggie-friendly restaurant in town, there is one thing you should consider: if you know how to cook, do it. Nothing is more appealing to another vegan than a prospective partner who knows their way around a kitchen. However, some vegans are picky eaters, so you'll want to find out what your date's likes and dislikes—for food. Find out about the *other* likes and dislikes later, unless you just plan on getting down to business.

If you're not quite a culinary genius, take heart. If I learned how to cook, so can you. You might even get good at it. When I became vegan the only thing I knew how to cook were eggs and bacon. Of course, being vegan, that presented me with some problems. After going on a tempeh binge for a few months, I was ready to try something new. Tofu was the next most promising option, but in the past I had been too scared to attempt the feat of cooking bean curd. People always say things like, "Tofu is so easy to cook, it just takes on the flavor of whatever you're cooking it with," or "it's like a canvas, and all you have to do is paint it with flavor." Bullshit. It's a pain in the ass to make tofu take on any flavor, at least for the novice vegan cook. You're going to need time, practice, and a whole bunch of Mrs. Dash. I promise this won't turn into a cookbook like every other fucking book about veganism, but here are some pointers, as nothing woos like the 'fu (alternately, "nothing says 'I wanna dry-hump you' like a steamy plate of tofu").

First of all, make sure you're cooking with the right tofu for your dish. There are a lot of different types of tofu. If you're really cooking it and not serving it raw or as a smoothie, you probably don't want silken tofu. Instead, go for the regular stuff. Like cocks, you can get it soft or firm, in varying degrees, depending on how you swing. For the best tofu, though, I always suggest finding a local Asian foods grocer, if you've got one nearby, as the stuff in the grocery store is okay, but not the best. Most of it is Naysoya™ (from the makers of—yuck—Nayonaise®). Bulk tofu from health food stores tends to be quite good if you aren't lucky enough to live near an Asian grocery. Oh, one more important thing: tofu at Chinese restaurants and at Asian grocers is normally referred to and labeled as Bean Curd, not Tofu. Don't worry, it's the same thing, although you can bet the stuff labeled "curd" is better. Want to make sure you find a good grocer? Talk to your favorite local Asian restaurants. It's likely they get their purchase orders from the same place.

What Not To Say On A First Date

1. "You know, I'm not wearing any underwear."
2. "Well, it's settled. This is going to give me the shits."
3. Anything about exes.
4. "My favorite movie? Oh, *definitely Waking Life*."
5. "How was I supposed to know that dog was going to run *right out* in front of the car? Sheesh."
6. "So, how much do I owe you?"
7. "How was I supposed to know those kids were going to run *right out* in front of the car after their dog? Sheesh."
8. "So, your sister/brother... How old is s/he again?"
9. "Spit or swallow?"

Still not sure you can pull it off? Don't have the time to learn the ways of the 'fu? Allow me to suggest pasta. It's hard to fuck that one up, even for you. Not only that, it's easy to pass yourself off as quite the gourmet. All you'll need is some nice olive oil (extra virgin, even if you're not), nutritional yeast, salt, pepper, and one or two fancy toppings. By fancy toppings, I don't mean bac'un bits and Vegenaise®. In fact, better not to mention your obsession with the V-goo until after you've been together awhile, and you know your partner can handle just how far it goes. No, in this case I'm referring to stuff like oyster mushrooms, artichoke hearts, kalamata olives, and sun dried tomatoes. The nice thing about these ingredients is they are available at pretty much any supermarket, in case you don't feel like dealing with the aging hippy feel-good fuckwad liberals down at your local co-opt.[4]

Does your date drink? This is something you'll want to know in advance. If your date happens to be an edger, you probably won't impress them much by busting out the whiskey the minute they step through the door. Get mineral water instead. Otherwise, be prepared with wine. And not just one bottle. You'll want a bottle of white and a bottle of red, because people are awfully picky about wine. Some will only like one sort or the other. So here's my suggestion: get a Chardonnay and a Shiraz.[5] It's hard to go wrong with either, and you'll probably get laid. On the other hand, if you get totally rejected, you can always drink all the wine, toss off, and when you wake up in the morning not remembering the previous night, *tell yourself* you got laid. In reality, the latter isn't quite as rewarding, but I promise you'll find it a surprisingly adequate substitute after the first few times.

So what exactly do you do on a vegan date? And what makes a "vegan" date, well, vegan? For some, it's as much about what you eat while you're dining as it is what you eat *after* you've dined (hint hint). For others, happiness is a warm pair of bolt cutters to raid a fur farm with your favorite tear gas cowboy/girl and then fleeing to Canaduh but calling it a "road trip." Where your ideal "vegan date" falls on the spectrum only you can say.[6] Then again, nothing is wrong with dinner and a movie. And here's my logic behind it: both activities give you plenty

---

4   Yes, the "t" in "co-opt" is a pun. I don't like co-ops that much. If you're the kind of person who needs explanations for everything, see my blog at thesmokingvegan. blogspot.com for more about why I don't like co-ops that much.

5   Keep in mind some wines and beers are not vegan, and may contain a range of animal ingredients from fish bladder derivatives to blood. For more information, see Animal Ingredients A-Z, or the resources page at veganfreak.com.

6   Immediately following this sentence there was, in my opinion, a really funny joke. But, one of my editor's didn't like it very much, so I'm erred on the side of good taste and deleted it. That said, I still think it's funny, so I'm going to post the text that

of time to root out the losers. For you, shitty taste in one or the other might be forgivable. For *no one* is shitty taste in *both* forgivable. What do they order for food? What movie do they want to see? After the movie, what did they think of it? For instance, I like to take my dates to steakhouses, just to see if they're tempted to get something other than the baked potatoes, or a sushi bar to see if they think fish is a vegetable, or if they stick to the avocado rolls. Then, I bring them to a porno theater. If an engaging discussion about just how *did* they get the camera *there* doesn't ensue, I can safely write that person off as a total weirdo.

If your date isn't vegan, and you're going out to eat, it's important you take them somewhere you can order something good. And I don't just mean passable, I mean *really good*. Even if there is only one menu option for you, it has to make them jealous they didn't order it too. This way, it shows them that maybe the whole "vegan thing" ain't so bad after all. If your date is a vegetarian, they may end up ordering an inadvertently vegan option as well if, for instance, you're at a Chinese restaurant. In that case, it's likely they'll end up with a tofu dish too. Either way, if your date isn't vegan, it can present some potential problems on the first outing. Let's expound.

Guilt. If your date is an omni, or even a veggie, there is a decent possibility they'll have some kind of guilt trip about consuming meat and/or dairy right in front of you. If they're ordering meat, it's possible they'll get all apologetic on your bitch ass, saying things like, "Sorry, I know this probably totally grosses you out," or, "It really must bother you to have to look at this meat." While there is no precisely tactful answer in a situation like this, I used to respond with a line like, "Oh, don't worry about it. My whole family eats meat. I'm used to it." Alternately, "No, I really don't care much what other people eat. I'm vegan but I don't expect everyone else to be. It's a personal choice," or, "Hey, it isn't my funeral." Unless of course their eating meat in front of you really *is* bothersome, in which case you probably shouldn't be on a

---

was supposed to be there on my blog after this book is published. That way, you can still see the joke, but I'm not making you pay for it. Fair? Fair.

date with them in the first place. If a situation like this comes up, it's your fault—after all, you knew that kind of thing bothered you but you asked them out anyway—and my advice is to lie. Lie like the dickens. Use one of the suggested lines, even if it's not true, and don't ask them out again.

If your date is a vegetarian, their feelings of guilt—if they have any— are apt to be slightly more complex. If they're a veggie for moral reasons, they may feel some moral shortcomings, or that you are morally superior to them for doing something which they feel they'd never be capable of. They may not say anything about it, but just because they don't doesn't mean they're not thinking it. It's important you don't contribute to these feelings. Try in subtle ways to dispel any guilty feelings by swallowing your pride and saying something quasi-complimentary about what they're consuming. Or not. That one is up to you. If your date is a moral veggie, there's a good shot they could make the full leap. That's why I recommend being accommodating, and also not discussing veganism on a first date, unless of course they ask about it. There's a decent chance they will, so be prepared to give non-offensive answers. The best way to handle a non-vegan is as though they have a big "fragile" stamp on their forehead. They probably don't know what you know. It doesn't make them morally inferior; people just progress in life at different paces. If their moral fiber is anything like your own, you probably don't need to worry much. Just give them time and understanding. If it's meant to be, they'll come around.

The Fine Art of Making of Out. Making out with a non-vegan can be a nightmare. If they're a vegetarian, or they've at least been eating that way around you, then it's probably not a big deal. But if they just had steak or fries smothered in beef gravy and cheese curds (Canucks call this *poutine*), you may be in for a bumpy ride—and not the sexy kind. This is probably the point at which you should strongly consider just how much this person means to you. I'm not saying dump their omni ass, just ask yourself if the pursuit is worth it. Any chance they'd consider becoming vegan sometime down the road? If not, maybe it's time to reevaluate the situation in a more realistic light. It's true some vegans can be with an omni long-term. Or at least, I've heard it's true. Hey, it may not be. But if such vegans really exist, I'm not sure how they do it. You'd have to ask them. You know, if they exist.[7] However, most vegans I know tell me they could never be in a relationship with a non-vegan. One or two have told me they could be with a vegetarian, but even that is too much for the majority of my vegan friends, as well as yours truly.

But let's say for the sake of argument—and because I'm getting paid by the word—that you still want to stick your vegan tongue down their omni gullet. Fuck, I'm not going to stop you. Is there a way to ensure you won't end up consuming an odd bit of mystery meat? Well, some meats (like steak) have a tendency to get stuck between one's teeth. So the answer is no, there's no way to ensure you're not going to end up consuming a little cooked dead animal flesh. Unless... Yeah, there is an unless. If your date is really understanding, they probably won't make you ask them to brush their teeth right after they eat—they'll just do it. If you're out and about, they'll at least make the effort to chew a stick of gum or have a breath mint. But your date may not like having to do this after the first few times, and if you make out a whole lot, as I suggest you do, then their toothpaste bill might start piling up. Still, I'm sure some omnis can be very accommodating about that kind of thing. Actually, "sure" isn't quite the word I was trying for; I think it would be more accurate to say "it's possible" some omnis can be very accommodating about that kind of thing. But I digress. (Did I mention I'm being paid by the word? Because I am.)

If your date *doesn't* have the good sense to have a stick of gum or brush their teeth frequently, then get ready for some shit dates. Nothing is worse than the oblivious omni. Perhaps this calls for an anecdote to help illustrate. No? Fuck yourself. I'm doing it anyway. And it all ties into the other possible nightmare scenario on a date with an omni:

---

7   I have it on good authority such vegans do, in fact, exist. You'll find more pertinent advice, some of it specifically tailored to your strange situation, after this chapter. In the meantime, hang in there!

Omni Stalkers. Kelly[8] is psychotic. To be fair—fair to myself, that is—I didn't know this when I met her. It was a normal night for me. I had been back in town for about a month at this point after returning from a several-month-long bunk attempt at a normal life in Montana. I guess I didn't realize there is no normal life in Montana. It's sort of important to my story here to mention that at this time in my life, I was, shall we say, a bit of an alcoholic. Not a diehard one, I didn't drink at work or anything. But like clockwork, after my day at the office, I would go home, get freshened up, withdraw some more cash from my increasingly lean checking account, and hit the B-town bars. I tried to cheer myself up with the nightly possibility that I might meet some cute vegan chick, particularly one with a penchant for whiskey like myself.

On this particular night, I found a girl with a penchant for whiskey, just not one who was vegan. Oh, and like I said, she was psychotic. Meet Kelly. Kelly is a slightly husky, occasionally pleasant and tolerable girl. The night I met her, I was with a friend at a semi-upscale bar and dance club populated mostly by irritating college students. Do I dance? You bet your literate ass I do! On that night, however, I was instead getting really, really plastered. I was despairing. As I stepped out onto the back porch to have a cigarette, my friend appeared with two girls. Apparently, he knew at least one of them from work. The other girl—I assumed he knew her as well—introduced herself as Kelly. I hesitate to say we hit it off, but we got along well enough, ended up chatting for a while longer, and sharing a few more cigarettes. Then the inevitable happened: she found out I was vegan. Not only that, she then explained to me about how she "used to be."

I should state up front I'm a little pissy about "ex-vegans." My philosophy is that if you aren't vegan now, you never were. I tried not to let this get my hackles up immediately, and the whiskey may have actually calmed me down a bit—not its normal impact on me. Rather than

---

8   All names have been changed so I don't get my ass sued. Or because I'm just that considerate. You decide.

leaving it at that, however, she went on, and it only got worse. Kelly proceeded to explain how now she eats everything, but only meat and eggs that are organic and locally produced. First of all, I had the sneaking suspicion that even this was bullshit. What was most irritating was that she clearly didn't seem to grasp the fact I didn't care. Of course I object to animals being pumped up with hormones and antibiotics, but you know what I object to even more? Killing them! If she couldn't wrap her mind around that one, I had a hard time believing she ever ate something remotely close to a vegan diet. If you're ever in a situation like this, now is when you should cut out. I, however, was way too drunk to try.

The entire time I executed with great precision my perfected nod-and-smile tactic, honed to a razor's edge—sharp enough to cut through granite as though it were Earth Balance—after years of experience during holidays and at non-alcohol-lubricated family functions. It seemed to work, but no matter how much I nodded and smiled she just kept talking about it, and talking about it, and talking about it. I couldn't tell if she was apologetic or just stupid. Just as I was about to explain that I only hear dietary confessions on Sundays, she tried to stick her tongue down my throat, a tongue that had presumably been helping to choke down whole assload of meat and dairy at some point earlier that very day.

It's hard to know exactly just what to do in a situation like this. Realistically, you've got a few options. But that's always in retrospect. While it's happening, you've really only got two options: go with it, or bust out your ninjitsu or your old-school Street Fighter moves, none of which I'm very good at because I liked Mortal Kombat better, and as far as I know it's probably illegal to rip someone's head off along with their entire spinal column. Sometimes, like when you've had a lot of whiskey, your brain can be a little hazy. In my case, I rolled with it. For about two seconds. That was before my brain, shocked out of nod-and-smile mode, realized I was under attack at which point I launched into my well-scripted "Gee, look at the time" spiel, also developed over the course of years of the same family events. Remember what I said about how omni chicks just don't get it? This is kind of what I'm talking about. Plus, *nothing* is worse than an "ex-vegan." The most you can ever expect in a relationship with an ex-vegan is an eventual ex-girlfriend. Ultimately, I explain that I don't want a relationship. I feel bad about letting people down, but sometimes enough is enough. Fast forward a few months.

I'm at an after-party for a cabaret show at another overpriced venue. In fact, I'm with the same friend that was with me the night I first met my omni stalker-to-be. On our way in, Kelly and a gaggle of her friends are waiting in line. At first it looks like they are actually going to get turned away, which made me feel pretty safe. But after about five minutes milling around inside, there they were. She approached and proceeded immediately to put her arm around me and start rubbing my back. The discomfort this created is something akin to every man's favorite part of getting your annual physical. The rest of the evening was spent dodging my new stalker.

After a series of close calls and minor disasters, including an assumption on her part that I had purchased her a beer, and an attempt—also on her part—to try and hitch a ride with my friend and me back to town, I finally snuck out the back exit of the venue. Figuring the evening was pretty much ruined, I thought we'd be going home. But my friend had heard of an after-after-party somewhere in the Old North End near both of our apartments. I thought I might be able to at least salvage some of the night, so I hesitantly agreed to tag along. Some people were there already, including a cute girl I had noticed at the original disastrous after-party. Someone bought some obnoxious bourgie Polish sweet-bread from New York and was cutting it up. When my friend asked if I wanted some, I declined, saying "It probably has eggs in it." Not a moment later does Lynn, the cute girl, also decline for the same reason. Exchanging fast glances, and sensing my interest, my friend plied for me, "Are you vegan?" "Yeah," she answered. Suddenly things were looking up. In the next ten minutes, I learned that Lynn was not only vegan, but her favorite drink was straight whiskey, her favorite comedian was David Cross, her favorite movie genre was Asian horror, and she smoked—a lot. A match made in heaven? Ultimately I'd never know, because that was when Kelly walked in the door.[9] Clearly, there was no stopping the stalker.

As I was sadly attempting to put the moves on Lynn, Kelly approached and began rubbing my back. Think it looked like I already had a girlfriend? *Yeah.* I told Lynn I was going to go have a cigarette, and she joined me. After some more uninvited touching from Kelly, I leaned into Lynn to explain I wasn't sure why this girl kept touching me, and that it was actually making me really uncomfortable. Phew, I thought. *Safe.* She knows I'm single. But by this time I couldn't stand the unwanted attention any longer. I had to leave. I excused myself, and left Lynn to the gathering throng of socialites that rather resembled insects on a porch bustling around the bug zapper. Not only was Kelly shaping up to be an obnoxious alcoholic stalker, she also fouled up my one chance with one of the only cool vegan girls I had ever met until that point. Actually, one of the only vegan girls I had met, period. Not only did omni chicks seem not to get it, they just downright sucked.

After a lot of thought about the incident, it hit me: these are the three main dangers anyone needs to accept when dating omnis: guilt, making out, and stalkers. If you can get past these hurdles, who's to say you might not succeed at finding love? Eventually even I did, but we'll save that story for later. You might not believe it, but there are more pertinent things you'll need to concern yourself with when it comes to dating, beyond stalkers—like talking.

Throughout your date, you're going to need things to talk about. In the adult world, we call this "conversation." In the dating world, I call it "buttering up" for sex, or, finding out for sure just how much of a winner or loser your date is. If you're dating a fellow vegetarian or an omni, you can expect some tough questions from them. Let's go over a few, and discuss how you might respond, since you've already paid for my advice and all.

---

9   This turned out not to be a bad thing. More later.

Why are you vegan? If you get this question during mealtime, I suggest putting off the discussion until later. Try something like, "Sorry, I don't usually talk about that while I'm eating." You can explain this away as just one your many lovable quirks. When you finally do get around to the topic, I suggest avoiding "you" language, such as "*You* shouldn't eat meat." When it comes time to really answer the heart of the question, be honest without giving them more information than they can process at once. Tell them you object to the concept of animals as property, that you cannot, in good conscience, support the animal cruelty industries, whatever. However, they don't need to hear about debeaking, docking, bolt guns, hydraulic scissors, and kill floors off the bat. That is, unless they ask. Then it's their fault. Chances are, they'll ask. And "I just don't like the way chickens are treated" isn't going to suffice for an answer. You may just have to get down and dirty. Some of my vegan friends would likely say this is a no-no, but I say fuck that. They've gotta hear it some time, and if they asked, then they asked.

Do you expect me to become vegan? You probably won't hear this question on a first date. But you might on a second or third, because it's bound to become an issue at some point. The truth is, you don't *expect* them to become vegan, but you sure *hope* they do. There's a big difference. One allows for a person's own agency, the other seeks to deny it. By the time you get this question, you'll probably be in a position to better gauge more accurately how you feel about the person. If you really like them a lot, then the answer needs to be "No, I don't expect you to become vegan." Don't even tell them you hope they'll become vegan. What works well in the bedroom doesn't work well when it comes to veganism: the hands-off approach is best if you really have any hope this person might do it. If they feel as strongly about you, chances are they're considering it already. Don't go fucking it up. In the meantime, you need to ask yourself a more important question; namely, is being vegan the most important thing you're looking for in a partner or not? Because if they don't eventually become vegan and you haven't considered this, you're going to find yourself stuck in an ugly little rut and facing some rather unpleasant choices. If they do decide to go vegan, or at least start making the transition, I'll have more advice for you in the next chapter, "Love, But Vegan."

Finally, there are a few other things you should consider as we close up the chapter on dating. As much as you're sensitive to your new partner's current non-vegan status, they need to be respectful of your status as a vegan. They don't need to put you on a pedestal for your choices or moral compulsions; if they do it's probably a bad sign they have some rather deep-seated insecurities about themselves and their personal choices, or just lack a broader sense of self. But they do need to honor the fact that you're vegan by not doing things like teasing you about being vegan, or arguing that you're "taking this whole animal rights thing too far" by not wearing wool or eating honey. Anything of this sort should be a big, fat red light, letting you know it's time to apply the brakes—hard. If the person you're seeing can't respect you being vegan, or deal with your veganism in an appropriate way, it's time to cut them loose, no matter how great they may be when they're not being an ass.

Well, it's time to wrap up the dating chapter. And how better to wrap it up than a discussion about what to do *after* a date, or,

Dessert. Let me state outright that I'm not generally known as a very conservative sort of guy. When it comes to relationships, however, I tend to see things a little differently than many of my friends and acquaintances. Perhaps I was just born in the wrong century. Allow me to explain. If you've just had a first date, I don't think getting your fuck on right after dinner and a movie is a good idea, even if you went to the porno theater together. It's an especially bad idea if you want or hope to have any sort of meaningful, lasting relationship. While I'll get into this more in the next chapter, a lot of my hesitancies in this regard stem from the way people treat each other in and out of relationships, and the way they treat animals as well. In other words, people treat each other like pieces of meat. If your are really digging on someone after a first outing, then respect them enough to wait. I'm not saying wait until marriage, but hell, is a week too much to ask? By actually getting to know someone first, at least on a semi-fundamental level, the sex is going to be exponentially better. Getting it on after your first outing is just going to be getting off. There's nothing wrong with getting off, but part of the whole point of finding someone else to share your life with is that they provide something your hand, vibrator, or removable adjustable shower head cannot. Even if it's not your style, suggest some soy ice cream for desert, and save the hot and heavy stuff for later. On a first date, a kiss will do just fine, maybe even one with some tongue. Follow this simple piece of advice, and you'll thank me later. It'll be worth it. I promise.

chapter **3**

Love, but Vegan

People in love represent a lucky minority of the world's population. Real love, I mean. Count yourself even luckier if your true love also happens to be vegan. But what if they aren't? Never fear. We'll deal with both scenarios together. I think you'll find they have much more in common than not.

Being in love is a wonderful thing, like a cute, fuzzy kitten. It can also be a remarkably shitty thing, like a cute, fuzzy kitten that pisses in your shoes, or sits on your chest as you sleep, trying to suck out all of your breath. Like cute, fuzzy kittens, sometimes you don't find out which sort of love you're in until a long way down the road. But in a way, that's part of the point of being in love. Either way you stack it, you're taking a risk. And it's a big risk. Bigger than gambling the title to your car, signing away your first born in blood for eternal life. It's that big of a risk because what you're risking isn't a car, maybe not getting eternal life as part of a Faustian bargain, or pissing away your money on a hacky virtuoso's latest audio swill, but rather *yourself.*

So there's some gravity to the whole "love" thing, the "L" word, or whatever you want to call it. Hell, most people have trouble even *saying it* to anyone but their parents. There are a few reasons for this, as I see it. One is the way we're taught to view each other. The other is the risk involved in love. As you may have noticed, I'm going to talk about the latter first.

People are incredibly isolated creatures. In a fundamental way, they are afraid of each other, and a lot of that fear has to do with acceptance, rejection, commitment, and responsibility by/to/for one another. We see others as untrustworthy at worst, and undependable at best. We are taught the only person you can rely on is yourself. Coupled with the potential for nearly unparalleled hurt that comes with love, why take the risk on a serious relationship with another potentially untrustworthy, undependable, inherently flawed person who might not keep a commitment to you? Someone who might now be responsible with your heart? *Because.* Because you're that person too. You are just as undependable, inherently flawed, and able to accept, reject, commit, respect and disrespect as the next person. As much as it might be nice to think it, and as much as it might be true in regards to things other than relationships, when it comes to love you are just as fucked up as everyone else, maybe more so. After all, you are reading this book, aren't you?

So let's take this love thing all apart, piece by piece. It's not as mechanical as I'll make it sound, but sometimes crude is effective.

Dependency. Love means depending on someone other than yourself. It means more than being able to depend on someone else; it means being able to *let yourself* depend on someone else. For some people this is easy, but for others it's not such a facile task. Some people relish their independence. There's nothing wrong with this, but if you're ever going to be able to really love, you'll have to realize (if you don't already) that part of being truly independent, as my friend Jenn Jarecki used to say, is realizing just how dependent you are on others, and accepting this as not a bad thing, a sign of weakness, or a loss of some former, ethereal "independence." Too often, people confuse being a loner with independence. Self-reliance isn't a sin. It's something everyone should have, and needs to have before they can love. But isolation and independence are different things entirely. People see their own confused definition of independence as "freedom," whatever that means. Freedom *of* something or freedom *from* something? What I mean is, freedom of self or freedom from others? "Freedom" is an awfully ambiguous word.

Would you rather be free to date dozens of people, endlessly drifting from one failed, meaningless quasi-relationship to the next? Or is a committed, enriching relationship—something that doesn't require all the searching and awkwardness of repeated relationships—more liberating and in a more meaningful way? These are questions you need to ask yourself. They are important questions. And if you cherish your right to be a player, as some of my acquaintances do, what kind of freedom is more important? The freedom to fuck whomever you want or the freedom to be your honest self for once with this whole other person who means the world to you?

Commitment. This one ties into dependency in many ways. A lot of my friends are commitment-phobes. As this is a proclivity I don't quite get, it can be at times difficult for me to analyze it with any real degree of accuracy, but I'll give it a shot. Being committed to someone other than one's self is an experience many people have not had, unless of course you have a child. And no, pets don't count, no matter how much you love them. Love for pets is different, like love of parents. Real commitment means loving something, or in this case some*one*, more than yourself. Some people mistake feelings like this as unhealthy. These people don't know love, and most probably never will. True commitment means being really devoted to something grander than yourself for once. As I noted, for a lot of people this is frightening. Only most of them won't 'fess up and say that's why. Instead, they think of other creative excuses, like "I just don't like to be tied down," or, "I value my independence too much" (see what I meant about how this ties into dependency?) Frequently, these same people will rarely even use the word commitment except in that sad, tired, hackneyed slogan, "I just don't think I'm ready for that kind of commitment." Friends, these sad specimens of humanity will *never* be "ready" for that kind of commitment, because not only are they utterly ignorant of just what real commitment means, they don't get that it's not about being "ready" for it. Unlike weekend drinking binges, pudding wrestling, or virgin sacrifice, there's no preparatory work to be "ready" for commitment. With love, commitment finds you, not the other way around.

Honesty. Honesty is a funny thing, and something most people aren't very good at due to how we relate to one another. People want to please each other, gain acceptance, and not rock the boat, which means not being your honest self with others. In a committed relationship, that's not going to cut it. Probably. I will say I know some couples who don't care that much about the whole "honesty" thing, and keep a lot of shit from each other. I think this is a recipe for disaster; they think it works, and believe there are some things they could never tell their partner or *would* never tell them. I think this is crap. It's cliché for sure, but if you don't have honesty then you don't have much of anything at all, let alone a real relationship. Still, for some people there is such a thing as being too honest. Basically this means how much they want or can deal with or process or whatever in the way of details. Classic example: exes. Invariably, whether you discuss them or not early on with your partner, exes are going to come up. After a lot of experience in this particular realm, I'd have to say I think it's best to get the ex discussion out of the way early on so there's no unpleasant surprises later. But how much does your partner want to know about you and your exes? How much do you want to know about them and theirs? Just that they dated someone? Or do you want to know what their sex life was like as well, so you can know how you stack up in the big picture? This might be a case of *too honest*, i.e., too much information, especially unnecessary information. But, some people can deal with that sort of thing. You need to figure out where you fit here.

Sometimes the commitment issues won't be on your end, but theirs. In some respects, as a vegan, it may be easier for you to commit to something big—and very long-term—than it is for other people. If you've been vegan for a long time, commitment in other contexts doesn't seem nearly so frightening.

A final note on honesty. Honesty also means communication. Communication is awfully hard without honesty. Lack of this factor will seriously hamper you and your partner talking about the important stuff of the relationship. If you can't communicate, your relationship will eventually end up on life support, comatose, or worse, just plain dead.

Trust. This is the baseline for any human relationship of any sort, but it is an absolute for the sort of relationship this book is about. It's also a funny thing, and I've found it changes over the years; or at least, perhaps my perception of it changes. For some people, trust is earned, not given. Others seem to be able to dole it out as they please. Many times, our ability or capacity to trust others is limited by past hurts, some of which can be incredibly difficult to overcome. In my case, this took the form of a long (for me, anyway) relationship of two years beginning in high school. Unfortunately, the majority of that two years was marked by what I'd like to imagine was an unusually high level of infidelity on the other person's part, contrasting a bit with my complete faithfulness. This made recovery extremely difficult, not only to feel anything for anyone again, but to trust anybody. I prefer to think I take one or two big lessons away from every failed relationship. This may or may not actually happen. Regardless, it took me awhile to figure it out, but I eventually learned it's unfair to bring baggage like that to a new relationship. When you haven't known someone long enough for them to "earn" your trust (today I'm not entirely sure what that even means), you've got to give them the benefit of the doubt. I realized that, for me, trust was a choice, something that could be given or withheld freely. Trust is what shores up a relationship despite any stormy weather it might encounter. Without it, you've got yourself a leaky boat that won't last long.

Monogamy. It seems to be a hard one for most people I've known, and even more unfortunately, most that I've dated. This could just be an age thing, though. If you're a person of middle age reading this, perhaps monogamy isn't an issue for you or your loved ones, and hasn't been in the past. If this is the case, good for you; you're lucky. I'll probably get the stick taken to me by the "free love" folks, but the joke's on them. There's very little "free" about love. It takes a lot of work, and even more commitment. "Hooking up" with a potpourri of partners may be free, but it sure doesn't constitute love. All the stuff you hear from people who ascribe to this banal tripe tends to amount to statements like, "One person could never be enough for me," or, "There's nothing wrong with loving more than one person." This is sheer smokescreen. It isn't that one person "could never be enough," it's that free love-types are afraid of actually giving themselves completely to some*one* else. Likewise, there's nothing wrong with loving more than one person, so long as we don't confuse what love means. I suppose it's fair to say love means a great many things to a great many people, but real love—the kind different than one feels for one's parents or close friends—however varied its definitions may be, is exclusive.

Non-monogamous relationships are generally called "open relationships." For a very small number of people, these work. For the majority of attempts, however, if they are "open," it's only for one person. Many times open relationships are proposed by one person in a hitherto monogamous relationship as a means of retaining the person they "really care about," but maintaining their "sexual freedom." The other person in the relationship reluctantly acquiesces, thinking it might be better to agree to share their partner than lose them entirely. Meanwhile, the whole "open" rot begins to eat away at whatever base the relationship initially had. This is why monogamy matters. For most people, if you want a healthy relationship, then there's only room for two. Cheating is still cheating, whether someone alerts their partner to the possibility ahead of time or not. There's no such thing as "fair warning" when it comes to infidelity. How do you know if an open relationship will work for you? Well, you're a big kid. You've got to figure that one out yourself.

In many ways, I think "open relationships," as distinguished by some extent from polyamory or polygamy, are phenomena rooted in capitalist social relations. They represent, in effect, an effort to forge a compromise between the way people view each other as commodities with the strong human desire to have a bond with one other person exclusively. As a result, "sex is just sex," and it can be had with anyone, but feelings of love are reserved for a specific singular person. The argument goes that if a relationship is truly strong and secure, that "meaningless sex" with other people shouldn't really matter. Aside from the fact this degrades and objectifies the persons outside of the relationship with whom "sex is just sex," I submit an opposing proposition: if a relationship is really secure, strong, and grounded, that sex—or more appropriately, making love—is a representative act of union and love between the two people. Sex is not simply "just sex," and there is no real desire for it outside of the relationship.

Respect and Admiration. In the movie *Trust*—a personal favorite of mine—the two main characters agree that love equals "respect and admiration" (hence, why I stuck them together instead of making separate categories). It may not be complete, but it's a pretty good definition, as those two words imply a whole lot of things. They probably seem unnecessary to even mention, as they are kind of implicit in love itself, but I think they warrant expounding. To respect and admire someone, you have to take the person as a whole. Everyone has shortcomings (we're all human[1]). It's part of the package. To love someone completely, you've got to do just that: love them *completely*, including their shortcomings, foibles, flaws, or whatever you want to call the stuff about them that just drives you nuts. Because without these things, the person you love wouldn't be whole, and certainly wouldn't be "the person you love." You need to respect not only the person, but also their flaws. Not only that, you've got to go the extra step of admiring them, flaws and all. In other words, you've got to love them because of, not in spite of, that stuff. What separates respect and admiration from the rest of these categories is that they've got to come naturally. These two aren't things you can work on like the rest, they've got to just be there. If they aren't, then you had better keep looking, or you're wasting your time. What if one of their "flaws" is that they aren't vegan? To me, this isn't really a flaw, at least not in the traditional sense of the word. Rather, I see it as a question of morality. Therefore, it's not something I'd say you need to love. But if you hope it will change, it might be something you need to accept, at least temporarily.

Faith. Faith is a lot like trust, and for a lot of people the two are hard, if not impossible, to separate. Faith, however, involves going above and

---

1   Unless you're into bestiality or zoophilia, neither of which I condone. I know you're vegan because you love animals, but "loving" them in the carnal sense is not okay.

beyond trust. In many ways, trust is Faith 101, and faith itself is a remarkably complex and ambiguous term. Trust can be proven, whereas faith means trusting what cannot be proven. In this book, however, I'm going to prune down the word a bit, and define it in the crucial context of support. A big part of faith is supporting someone through everything, no matter what, even on those occasions—and they will occur—when that person loses faith in themselves. In this case, to have faith in someone is to have an unshakeable confidence in them and their abilities.

Reciprocity. All of these things I've hacked apart here are well and good, but worthless without reciprocity. You may only get out of something what you put in, but in relationships, its got to go both ways. Reciprocity is more than who spoons who.[2] It means you may feel all these ways about your partner, but they've got to feel the same way about you. This is where things tend to get tricky. If you can check off all these things with regards to your feelings towards your partner, that's great. But if the same can't be said for them, you're probably in deep shit. If you've got the whole communication thing down, now would be the time to use it. Figure out which of these things is lacking, and work like hell to fix it. If you succeed, your relationship will be all the stronger for it. If you don't, at least you tried, and that's important. It may not be much of a consolation, but sometimes it's part of the harder realities of life. The important thing is to keep trying, and keep your chin up.

---

2   Don't get me wrong here. If you're not ever getting the inside of the spoon, then your partner might just suck. If they don't like spooning at all, this is a big tip they may actually be frigid, soulless, one of the undead, a Nazi sympathizer, or just a Republican.

All of these things amount to a whole lot of risk, probably more than you've taken in your whole shitty, pathetic, lame, heretofore worthless excuse for a life.[3] But what have you got to lose?[4] Exactly.[5]

Signs they aren't into you

1. They don't return your calls.
2. They cover you with sirloins while you sleep.
3. One by one, all of your pets begin to die mysteriously.
4. They got drunk and crashed your car.
5. They send you "love notes," which are actually envelopes devoid of any real letters, but containing only a handful of razor blades.
6. They send "coming out" cards to all your family members for you (unless you're actually already out).
7. They laugh when they hit you.
8. They won't introduce you to any of their friends or relatives.
9. They just want to hang out "alone" all the time.
10. They say things like, "I'm not into you," "I don't like you," "You smell," or "I'd rather fuck a 90-year-old virgin for money."

The First Part Last

At the beginning of this chapter, I also said part of the reason people have so much trouble with the whole "love" thing is the way in which we view each other. Fair warning, though: there's a decent chance you

---

3   Yeah, I know I'm being unduly harsh here. Sorry. Actually, I'm not. But really, I am. You know, in a "not sorry" kind of way. Am I kidding right now? I might be.

4   Aside from your friends, dignity, and self-respect, that is. (Don't worry, you probably won't lose any of these things, and if you do, it's probably worth it.)

5   Okay, really, I promise to take a break from the excessive footnoting for at least a page. Cross my heart.

may find this portion of the chapter intensely boring compared to the prior half. Still reading? Well, like I said, fair warning.

In many, if not all respects, capitalism shapes and cuts the lens through which we view one another. As our old friend Uncle Karl[6] contends—and I agree with him—capitalism has turned us into fundamentally alienated beings. What's left in human relationships is highly routinized and heavily scripted. People relate to each other like business models, commodities, or through comparison to movies and books. You'll often hear friends describe an event with the statement, "It was like this one episode of [insert TV show here]..." People are described as "a good match," "a great team," "synergistic," etc., all business language and all phrases one might use, as my friend Bob suggests, to describe a corporate merger. Capitalism raises us to compete with and fear each other, while love is relegated to the second aisle from the left in the Hallmark shop.

When people treat each other like commodities, you're never going to see a healthy relationship. What I mean is, when it comes to relationships, all too often people view others like objects, not subjects; they view others like a new pair of shoes, a video game, a car, or an iPod. When the next, newest model hits the market, the old one gets tossed. *Getting tired of your old pair of shoes? This new model is even better! Get rid of those old shoes, and buy yourself the newer, different, more exciting pair! After all, you've earned them! You* deserve *them.* This sound familiar at all? It should. *Tired of your current boyfriend/girlfriend? Have you seen the newer, hotter item? Maybe they'd make you happier. Too bad trade-ins aren't offered, it looks like you'll just have to hump 'em and dump 'em!* Does anyone else see anything wrong with this picture?

Erich Fromm described the origins of this sort of relationship in the commodity form in his 1956 classic, *The Art of Loving.*

---

6   Marx, that is. Shit. I broke my promise didn't I? Then again, I didn't expect anyone to read the second half of the chapter anyway, so you probably didn't notice. Ha.

At any rate, the sense of falling in love develops usually only with regard to such human conditions as are within reach of one's own possibilities for exchange. I am out for a bargain; the object should be desirable from the standpoint of its social value, and at the same time should want me, considering my overt and hidden assets and potentialities. Two persons thus fall in love when they feel they have found the best object available on the market, considering the limitations of their own exchange values. Often, as in buying real estate, the hidden potentialities which can be developed play a considerable role in this bargain. In a culture in which the marketing orientation prevails, and in which material success is the outstanding value, there is little reason to be surprised that human love relations follow the same pattern of exchange which governs the commodity and the labor market.

You can treat people like commodities, like there's a "newer and better," but it doesn't make it so (you know, unless you are a filthy capitalist pigdog). This attitude can probably be summed up by the colloquialism "The grass is always greener on the other side." Perhaps things are different for my older audience, but younger people today seem intent on never sticking anything out, let alone relationships. If one requires work, then something must be wrong with it. Good relationships are supposed to be easy all the time, right? Relationships aren't like a pair of shoes, cars, or any other sort of commodity in many ways, but in one very important respect—when they don't function "the way they're supposed to," it doesn't mean it's time to get a new one, or that the new one will necessarily be any better. People who view relationships in this fashion will drift from one to the next, and never be happy.

This isn't to say you should always stick it out. Of course relationships can really go bad, beyond the point of repair. This is often the case with infidelity, and always the case with physical and mental abuse. The problems relationships encounter are too broad, varying, and dependent on the individual relationship itself to explain, explicate, or diagnose in one book such as this, but the easiest litmus test to administer to determine whether your relationship is past fixing is whether or not one of the basic aspects of love I outlined earlier has been mostly or entirely eroded. If this is the case, it may be time to put yourself–to use another great ironic invention of capitalist phraseology in regard to relationships—"back on the market."

If there are problems, but none of these major aspects of love have been eroded, there's an extremely good chance the relationship can be saved and made stronger. This perhaps sounds formulaic, and I don't mean it to; this is meant more as a general sort of guideline. Nothing works one hundred percent, all of the time. However, to fix something like a relationship requires *work*, something many people seem unfortunately reluctant to actually put into them. Part of this problem has to do with the way love and relationships are portrayed culturally. We see movies and read books in which relationships are perfect storybook loves, the only conflicts coming from primarily external sources. For better or worse, in real life this is simply not the case. Truly good relationships rarely come easy, and even when they do, they never stay easy. There will always be hard times, and like so much else in life, ultimately it's up to you to decide when they're irreparable. Is it time for me to open all up again?

Here's where I open all up, again

After my failed high school-to-college relationship, I needed to do some serious reevaluating, to figure out what went wrong, when and where. The most obvious answer to that question was when she started cheating on me. While there may have been other problems in the relationship, I figured this was by far the most serious and what made things impossible to fix in the end. I decided at that point that if I ever saw any of the telltale signs of infidelity again in any future relationship, I would bail immediately and spare myself the hurt. I thought, at that time, the most important thing in a relationship was trust, and any other problems not having to do with this could be fixed. In retrospect, this was too easy of an answer, and ultimately proved dreadfully wrong.

Enter Jess. After a year or so of really unsuccessful dating, I met her. We had gone to the same high school together, but were separated by a few years; as a result I hadn't known her in high school, and we met through someone who was, back then, a mutual friend. I liked her a lot from the outset, but I can't say that feelings were quite mutual. What made my sad pursuit of her even more pathetic, it seemed, was the fact that she was a lesbian coming out of a year-and-a-half long relationship largely torn apart by a lot of cheating. So we had that in common—cheating women, that is—and also, she was a vegetarian. Yeah, I was vegan, but I figured I wouldn't limit myself so much as to exclude an ethical veggie[7].

I met Jess in the summer after my sophomore year of university, and we hit it off—as friends. We hung out on a nearly daily basis, watched a lot of movies together, and found a bunch of mutual interests, one of which was apparently not each other. After some time, however, that began to change, and I became what she referred to as her "exception"— to women. All told, we were together what was just days short of two and a half years.

A lot happens in two and a half years. Not so long into the relationship, she became vegan of her own accord, for which I was enormously proud of her, as her favorite and often only foods prior to this shift had consisted of microwave cheese pizzas and egg salad sandwiches. I got my driver's license just before returning to university the summer after we met, for the express purpose of being able to drive the three and a half hours nearly every weekend back home to see her (I had held out for a long time on the driver's license thing). My junior year of college we got a dog together, a beautiful redbone coonhound named Guinness, who she and her mother took care of while I was away at school. Things seemed to fly by from that point on, until we hit Montana. But perhaps that's jumping ahead a bit much.

Not too late into the relationship I noticed some problems. However, one of those problems was not infidelity, so I figured the rest of them could probably be fixed, and maybe they weren't that big anyway. After all, I brought plenty of flaws and shortcomings to the table myself. My

---

7   As much of a contradiction in terms I think that is.

hygiene regimen, to put it generously, sucks. I have an awful memory, which includes forgetting birthdays[8], changing my rats' litter,[9] doing my laundry, changing my car oil, cleaning of any sort (dishes, room, self), paying bills on time,[10] etc. There are a bunch of other stupid, dumb, occasionally hurtful, and usually crappy things I do, which I'm sure Jess would be more than happy to outline here were I to grant her the space in this book.[11] Suffice it to say, I never considered myself the pick o' the litter, "a real catch," the best thing out there, Hashem's "gift to women," or any other sort of bizarre self-aggrandizement or accolade.[12] Really, I still think I pretty much suck, and am totally intolerable either to date or live with, for a variety of reasons. I don't think any of these problems make me an inherently bad guy, just not dating material, that's all.

Jess, by comparison, had very few shortcomings. She was, and I suspect still remains, sharp, intelligent, pointed, uncompromising, and deeply caring about social injustice. It's important to me to highlight these points so you don't think much less of her for the rest of what I'm about to write.[13] Because in the end, I think she may have suffered from one of the same shortcomings—"not relationship material." In her case, this was manifested in temperament, which was, well, her temper. On this one point, I suspect she'd scarcely disagree.

---

8   Sorry, Mom. Dad's is just much easier to remember, probably because it's April Fool's day. Couldn't we just move yours to Halloween or something?

9   My rats at the time, Marx and Engels, did not appreciate this.

10   Or in some cases, at all.

11   Obviously, I'm not going to do this. You'll probably see why in the next page or so. Oh, did you notice? I went a page without footnotes. Yeah, not this page, but like two pages before it. Anyway, back to the book.

12   My mom, as well as Jenna, would probably disagree with this. For the record, my mom has always told me I'm a "clothes horse," whatever that means (apparently clothing looks good on me, which is good, as I'm not a nudist). Neither, however, would disagree with existence of my shit memory and my total inability to do anything required of the rest of the adult world in even the most basic sense (laundry, bills, etc.).

13   Also, my publisher tells me we can't really afford a lawsuit. But also so you don't think much less of her.

It was bad. Not kind of bad, or sort of bad, or livable bad, but really bad. As in, *exceptionally bad*. It was also almost entirely erratic. In many cases, the slightest thing could set it off, and I'd have no idea until it happened what that thing was. Unfortunately, it usually seemed to be me. I figured it wasn't that big a deal, as she wasn't physically violent, just verbally. But that changed on several occasions, when I either had things thrown at me (ranging from portable phones to shoes), got hit, and in one instance was tackled to the floor and administered a pretty severe thrashing.[14] In retrospect, none of the physical stuff was as bad as the verbal. She knew how to use words to great effect, an ability that proved to cut both ways. In her more hysterical moments, she would take a great many things told to her in confidence, mostly deep-seated personal insecurities, regrets, fears, or shortcomings, and turn them against me in a manner that could only be called masterful yet deeply sadistic and psychologically traumatizing.

Like I said, though, I thought it was something we could overcome. Her temper started manifesting itself fairly early on in the relationship, and I remembered she had warned me after we first go together that it could get bad. I started to see just how bad, however, in her interactions with her mother and older brother. Minus the physical stuff—to the best of my knowledge—she executed precisely the same verbal assault tactics on them that she would later use continuously on me. It was startling, to say the least. In the end, it was as though she could transform in to this completely different being, composed entirely of rage and vengeance, at the drop of a hat. But it would only happen to those she allowed close to her. The cynical part of me thinks this was because she had to allow someone to get close enough so she could learn their individual psychology well enough to turn it against them later. The better part of me knows this is may be a grossly unfair speculation. To this date, I'm still not sure which is right.

Then came Montana. I was about to graduate from university, but she was in her freshman year. She was at a small liberal arts college in

---

14 I'm not very good at defending myself. In fact, I'm an incredible weakling.

a big city she hated in order to get her marks up enough to transfer to a better school somewhere else. After some debating over whether or not I would go to graduate school in Missouri, where I was accepted, or follow her out west where her transfer was accepted, I decided on the latter. We had put in so much time and work into the relationship, it didn't make sense to me to do anything else. But then again, that's just where my priorities tend to lie; not in career goals or opportunities, but in my relationships with others. At least in Montana we could have the life together we had been waiting for, or so I thought.

From the get-go in Montana, things were not good. After the first week in our apartment without the furniture having arrived, and knowing no one but each other, things began to deteriorate pretty quickly. Finally, she told me things just weren't going to work, and we should cut our losses. My parents booked me a flight home and tried to console me to the best of their abilities. But once she realized I was serious, and would really be leaving for good—and perhaps more importantly, the thing we had put so much energy into would be gone forever—she broke down, and pleaded the case for me to stay. I told her I wanted to stay, and would, but on one condition: she sincerely work on her temper, and if that meant getting professional help, she would. To my surprise, she agreed, and I called my parents to cancel the plane tickets.

For a while, things seemed to really get better. Her temperament seemed to change overnight, the furniture arrived, her classes started, I found a job, and we even made some friends. Granted, not many friends, and my shit job earned a measly six dollars an hour, but the relationship seemed better. By the holidays, it was becoming increasingly clear that our little renaissance was not going to last. Her temper had come back with a vengeance, and with Christmas break coming up at her university, she would have a month off. For that entire month, she would be home back east, whereas I would be home only for the week of Christmas to New Year's, and alone in our apartment the rest of the time. To make matters worse, things were light at work, and for the majority of that break I wasn't getting any hours, which meant no pay and plenty of time to be utterly alone. Lastly, shortly before that December, a very dear friend of mine committed suicide. We had planned to get together around the holidays, but it seemed that wasn't going to happen, at least not in the context we had imagined at the time. All of this left me very, very depressed.

For the month she was away, I barely heard from Jess. Even when our dog got sick, I had a wretchedly difficult time tracking her down to figure out what to do. I tried to channel most of the depression into something productive, like making music, as opposed to something unproductive, like wasting the last of my money at the nearby gas station video casino and liquor store, but somehow I managed to accomplish both. Drinking out of depression is not something I'd ever been prone to before, but that seemed to change that month. Even for the week I was home, I barely saw Jess, and when we did, she would fly into a rage about something totally banal. When she got back to Montana, it was clear things were different.

She had been harassing me, along with my parents, for months about grad school applications. Either I could go to the school she attended for my masters, but not a PhD, or go somewhere else she would later attend, for a continuous PhD program. Remember that thing about my bad memory? Well, I missed some application deadlines. My parents weren't very happy about this, but to my surprise, Jess was even less enthusiastic about the thought of my staying with her in Montana another year. Then it dawned on me: she didn't want me to stay. She wanted me to leave, as a pretext to break up with me. And until I left, she'd just hide her machinations, and let me think everything was fine. I may lack a lot of things, but being perceptive isn't one of them. After I told her the game was up, she sat in silence for a while on the bed, and then proceeded to inform me that "we've changed."

This was news to me. Aside from a depressing holiday season, I wasn't sure what exactly had "changed." What she meant to say, I interjected, was that *she* had changed. In any case, she explained, she didn't love me as much as she used to. Just how little? Well, I found out later that week while she was on the phone with the same friend that introduced us. Not at all, she said. After what was probably the worst and most exhausting fight in the history of our relationship, I locked myself in the bedroom—a favorite tactic of hers I took particular joy in turning around—and fell asleep. I awoke the next morning to banging on the door, and an announcement that it was over, and I was leaving. This time, for real.

It took a week to pack my stuff and mail it out, transfer the bills, and break my portion of the lease on the apartment, but I was out for good, and headed to North Carolina to get my feet back on the ground with a friend of mine already living there. During that week, she realized–again–that I was really leaving, and asked me to stay. But not as a partner, this time. I explained that wasn't going to work, and I needed to leave. After a lot of tears and my consolation that week, she drove me to the airport and I was on my way. Before I left, she had asked if we could stay friends[15] and stay in touch. I told her I didn't think that was a good idea, at least for a while, and she began sobbing until I finally acquiesced and told her I'd give her my cell phone number when I bought one in the Carolinas. Really, though, what was I going to do? I was torn. I still loved the girl even though I felt like she had put me through the wringer, and as shitty as things were, I still wanted her to be happy. I guess I'm just a sucker.[16]

As I suspected, the "friends" thing didn't exactly work out. Less than a week after my leaving, and on my encouragement, she went out to a party at a friend's place. I thought it would be good for her to get out, although in retrospect I'm unsure of why, at that time, I was concerned at all with what was "good" for her. Clearly, our entire history had meant so much to her, and she was really broken up about my leaving, so much so that she—in her words—"hooked up" with some random guy at that very same party. Oh, and then omitted that later

---

15 This is always a bad idea. Why do girls do this? I don't mean to generalize, but most of the guys I'm friends with would never stay in touch with an ex.

16 My friend Bob Torres, Bob's Jenna (as we call her), and my Jenna (as we call her) would probably say this is because I have a big heart. That's because Jenna gives me too much credit. Really I was just a sucker.

the same night when she called me in tears because she "missed me" and felt traumatized by the way all the guys at the party kept coming on to her. That was the end of the "friends" trial I offered her. After that, I received a couple of emails, and a letter. In the letter, she said she'd be home that summer to bring my rats back to me. In the follow-up email, she said she was moving out of the apartment, couldn't take the rats with her, was giving them away, and ended the email with the pleasant suggestion to, "fuck [me] and [my] life." I changed my phone number[17] and set my junk mail filters to her address. Thankfully, that was that last I heard from her.

During the entire course of the relationship, however, she never once cheated on me. She maintained this even after her immediate post-relationship "hook up,"[18] and of all the things she told me when we were together, this is probably the one I still believe to this day. The point in this whole story? Trust isn't the only thing you need to hold a relationship together. In effect, it's probably one of the big things I took with me on that plane. And, trust isn't as simple as infidelity. Trust should have meant I could trust someone, for example, not to turn my deepest insecurities on me when they were angry about something. In that respect, maybe the one element of trust wasn't even really present. As I said, I'm a sucker.

Aside from trust, everything else I outlined earlier was missing from the relationship on one of our parts or another, or both. Clearly, there were some respect issues. There was little or no reciprocity. Commitment and dependency were lacking. Whatever else, it was missing. In retrospect I simply confused monogamy with trust, and it was an error I paid for dearly. I lost everything when that relationship ended—my

---

17 This is always a good idea after a relationship ends. I don't care how many people you still want to talk and need to go through the pain in the ass of giving the new number to, it's worth it.

18 I should mention how much I hate this phrase. It's just fucking awful. Are people really such self-admirers or so totally ashamed that they can't simply say "I fucked around with a complete and total stranger?" I would probably never judge someone for that, nor would most anyone else. Using a euphemism like "hooking up," however, I do judge. I detest euphemisms.

job, my apartment, the new friends I had made, my dog, my rats, and what felt like the little dignity I had left. This isn't to say she didn't lose anything either. She lost much of life as she had known it, and I'm sure the transition wasn't an easy one for her. But it's not something I lose sleep over.

I'd like to think part of the reason I stayed around so long wasn't because she was vegan and the thought of starting over seemed insurmountable, especially if veganism might be a prerequisite. In my rarer moments of introspection and self-honesty, however, that was probably a pretty big reason, and also a pretty stupid one. I wonder how many other vegans have made the same mistake.

Hopefully if you've made it this far in our little adventure into all things vegan and love, you haven't wrapped your toes around a shotgun yet. Hopefully my last little bit wasn't *too* depressing. The point of this book, after all, is to encourage, not discourage you. If you're starting to feel discouraged, then keep reading. Things always start looking up, and from here on out things are generally on the up-and-up. Just remember—love consists of a great many things, far more than I mentioned in my neat little outline. But without those fundamental things, you ain't gonna have it. I know all of that sounds like a tall order, but I promise it's not an impossibility. In fact, once you open yourself up enough, you'll find all sorts of things are possible.

Even when you've got all I mentioned, love still takes work. If you're committed to doing it, and you know it's worth it, then you'll get out even more than you put in. But part of love means loving yourself, too, and knowing when you're in a bad situation. Sometimes, calling it quits is like a mercy killing. Only you can say when too much is too much, but the best way to be sure is to draw a mental line in the sand before you reach that point, and stick to your guns if and when you reach that line. Even if you lose everything else, you'll still have your dignity because you stuck by and were true to yourself. If you have a really healthy relationship, though, you probably needn't worry about ever reaching that line.

chapter 4

Meet the Parents: The Vegan Long-Term Relationship

Remember how I said dating is for losers? Well, eventually you'll get tired of being a loser, living alone in your apartment, cooking tofu for one, and listening to emo.[1] Sure it's nice to have your own space, but everyone (well, most people) reach a point where it's time to move upward and onward, to bigger and better things. If you've been seeing someone for awhile, and you're starting to feel like living between their place and yours is getting a bit strenuous, it's distinctly possible you are smack in the middle of the much dreaded, much maligned "Long-Term Relationship" (LTR). The good news is, there's nothing to be afraid of, no matter what the hype.

In this chapter, we're going to go over the nitty-gritty of the LTR. Think of it as a sort of survival guide, not that LTRs necessarily require any kind of "survival," *per se*. Let's take things one step at a time.

---

1   Or, if you're a bit older, Air Supply albums.

59

Getting Serious

Sometimes it's hard to get perspective on something you're deeply involved in. It's even harder when that very lack of perspective prevents
you from knowing just how deep you're in it. So maybe this will be of
some use.

Four signs things are getting serious:

The "L" Word. No, not the shoddy *Queer As Folk* knock-off. Here I'm
talking about "love." If you've said your I-love-yous together, and in
this case "love" corresponds to my little recipe cooked up in the last
chapter, things have definitely moved beyond the stage of just seeing
each other.

Post-infatuation Infatuation. All relationships start out with a period of normally intense infatuation. If it's been more than a few months
or a year and that total and overwhelming infatuation hasn't ended like
it has with every other relationship you've been in, then you're doing
more than just dating.

The Post-infatuation Goodness. The whole "infatuation period" may
end, but don't take this to mean things aren't serious as a result. Sometimes one of the most wonderful parts of a relationship can be when
the period of overwhelming infatuation ends, and your love for this
person is more intense than ever. This is when you're really getting
to know the person, beyond the rose-colored lens of infatuation. If
they're still everything you hoped for and more when you wake up
next to them in the morning, you're experiencing what I like to call
"the post-infatuation goodness." If you make it this far in a relationship, and this experience lasts, you may have sealed the deal.

The "V" Word.[2] If the person you've been seeing wasn't vegan but
became vegan since you've been seeing them, things could be *really*
serious. This depends, I've found, on the motives for the person becoming vegan: did they do it for you, or did they do it for animals
and their own ethics? Becoming vegan when you're in a relationship

---

2   Don't you wish there was a show about your everyday vegans with this title?

isn't like converting from one religion to another–or from no religion to a certain one—for someone else. The person has to do it of their own volition, and for reasons *other than you*. This not only assures that they'll most likely stick to it, but that they're mature enough to commit to something bigger than themselves on their own, and so most likely stick to you. If they became vegan for purely sycophantic[3] reasons, it's not a guarantee things are going to fail; it's just a better sign if they come to it own their own, for themselves, without any coaxing or pressure from you.

If you've experienced any or a combination of these four things, there's an excellent chance things have gone and gotten serious, maybe without you even really knowing it. If any of the stuff we're about to get into has already happened, then things are already serious, and I can't see any way you wouldn't know it.[4]

Meet the Parents

Meeting the parents of the one you love can be one of the most stressful experiences in the history of an LTR short of marriage, pregnancy scares, child rearing, or that time you return the "wrong tape" to the video store. That's because all of those things don't amount to other people judging you. Well, all but the "wrong tape" scenario.[5] The key difference then becomes that this person's parents might someday be in-laws. If you're lucky, you'll never hear about the tape again.

While parents, like most people, are too varied for me to offer any advice of particular specificity, there are some general rules you should follow if you want them to like you. If you don't really give a shit if they like you, you can ignore most or all of these. Most of them are probably no-brainers anyway.

---

3   In this context, the word sounds harsher than I mean it.

4   Unless you're a total fucking idiot, or just completely inept. But I'm banking on this not being the case. Oh, or unless the "person" you've been "seeing" is actually a tranny blow-up doll named Wendy. Sorry, Bob, s/he doesn't count.

5   I suppose a video store clerk, upon viewing the tape, could judge you as having given a fairly poor or unconvincing performance, which would be pretty bad.

Mind your manners. Say please and thank you. Avoid phrases, words, expressions, or conversational material—especially at the dinner table—such as fuck, fuckbag, fuckwit, motherfucker, dumbfuck, shit, shiteater, shit-eating, shitty-ass, jizzbag, whoremaster, pearl necklace, anal beads, anal leakage, goatse, tubgirl, donkeypunch, munging, cum dumpster, twat, bloody twat, piss up a rope, tea bagging, genital warts, Cleveland steamers, diarrhea, bloody diarrhea, explosive diarrhea, explosive bloody diarrhea, cocksucker, rusty trombone, cum stains, dirty sanchez, chocolate starfish, dry humping, and Franco-German disputed territories of Alsace and Lorraine. Also, if your partner's parents are divorced or one is deceased, avoid references to weddings, happy couples (even yourself), divorce, infidelity, death, fuzzy kittens, fuzzy dead rotting kitten corpses, or fuckbags generally. *Always* avoid anything having to do with veganism. This is worse than all other phrases, words, expressions, conversational topics or references combined—unless their parents are vegan, in which case, talk all you want about it. But still leave the other stuff out.

It's not as though they won't find out you're vegan. God knows it will make any dinner dates much easier if they know ahead of time. But just as it's rarely a good idea to discuss veganism on a first date, discussing it with your partner's family on a first dinner or outing may not be wise. Just make sure they know what you will and won't eat; something I'd leave to your partner to clue them in on.

And just to make sure we're clear, *don't swear*, and if you really want to play it safe, don't take the Lord's name in vain, either.[6]

Lie like fuck-all about the food. Unless your partner is vegan and has been long enough for their parents to learn how to cook vegan food, chances are any food prepped by said parents will *suck ass*. And that's being generous. Say things like, "This is amazing!" when what you really mean is, "I'd rather suck the sweat off a dead dog's balls than eat the rest of this!" or—if you really want to impress— "Would you mind sharing the recipe for this?" when what you really mean is, "How in the

---

6   Yes, I am totally for real on this one.

world did you manage to concoct something actually *more grotesque* than explosive bloody diarrhea on a plate?" If you're having a really difficult time choking the food down, try not breathing through your nose whilst eating—this will prevent you from actually tasting ... well, whatever it is they're serving you/trying to kill you with. Sometimes you just gotta take one for the team, so to speak. Dinner with your partner's parents is one of those times.

There is, of course, the possibility your partner didn't tell their parents in advance that you're vegan, or that no matter how explicit your partner was about what that does/doesn't mean, their parents still didn't quite get it. This can make for some pretty uncomfortable situations. At times like this, you're left with two choices: eat something you know isn't vegan so you don't risk offending them and then deal with being more explicit about veganism later, or be up front. Frankly, I think the latter approach works best if you do it sensitively. Say, "That looks really good, but I can't actually eat [insert animal product]." As long as they made something else like salad, you can reassure them that you've just eaten anyway (even if this is a lie), and the salad will be fine—no need to worry, you appreciate their efforts. After dinner, drive to the nearest Subway. Note the use of the word "can't" in the previous example. Don't say that you "don't," or even worse, "won't" eat something. That can seem snobby. Can't implies something might happen if you do eat it—and something might. Finally, if this approach won't work for you, but you still won't eat what's been prepared, practice at home for the following: the napkin trick. This is when you wait for a moment when the host/parents are occupied, then quickly shove as much as you can of whatever it is you ain't gonna eat into your napkin. Then politely excuse yourself and head to the bathroom, napkin in tow, where you promptly flush said offensive dish.

Come bearing gifts. This is a nice, polite gesture, showing them that you are a nice, polite young man/woman, even if this may be a particularly deceptive image for you to cast of yourself. The important thing is that they never get to know *the real* you. Anyway, if they drink, bring wine or nice beer.[7] If they don't drink, bring some artisan bread.[8] If they're on the Fatkins diet or some variation thereof, and neither drink *nor* eat bread, bring a cyanide capsule implanted inside a hollowed-out molar just in case you find yourself unable to make it through the first few hours around them. Your local dental hygienist can do this simple procedure, but make sure to book ahead!

Laugh at jokes, even when they're not funny. And they won't be. Probably none of them will be. Also, if you're not sure if what they said was a joke or not, look for visual cues from their spouse or other relatives nearby, such as the "Huh, huh? Whadda ya think of *that?!*" eyebrows coupled with a shit-eating grin. Pay attention to body language. If it looks like what was just said was meant as a joke, then laugh. If you're still not sure, just kind of smile and chuckle. If it turns out it really wasn't a joke at all, try to change the conversation as quickly as possible to cover your tracks.

Sometimes the joke thing can be difficult, when the jokes are not only *not funny*, but downright distasteful. If their humor has unpleasant, off-color, or backwards racial or gender proclivities, for example, you'll need to decide how to handle the situation. I'm not going to suggest you should play along with or be a party to shit humor, however, sometimes it can catch you so off-guard you're not really sure what to do. In circumstances like this, it's best to pretend they didn't say anything at all, and once again, politely try to shift the conversation somewhere north of Hell. If they're stubborn, this can be hard, but you won't find yourself left with a great many options. Occasionally confrontation works, but normally you should leave that to your partner.

---

7   Nice beer, people! This means NO BUDWEISER. Try a German beer. They're vegan by law, and well-priced. It's hard to go wrong with a German beer. Oh, and as for the wine, bring something on the cheaper side. If you bring something too expensive, it'll look like you're sucking up. Just bring something pleasant, like Yellowtail or Black Swan brands.

8   Don't go cheap on the bread, but stay simple. What I mean is, no Wonderbread, but you won't need a fancy loaf of Jewish Rye either. Just go for a couple of nice baguettes.

This is often a bigger problem with grandparents, but the point is, you should be ready for anything.[9]

Just be yourself. By which I mean your *best* self. By which I mean, for the love of God, don't be yourself. The first time around, at least, be whatever you think they want you to be. If it's a yuppy fuckbag social-ite, fine. If it's a slack jawed yokel redneck, do it. The idea here is to pin down their personalities as quickly as possible, and then emulate them to the best of your abilities. This way, they'll feel comfortable know-ing their son/daughter is in your capable similar-to-theirs hands. Just don't get caught faking it, or you're pretty fucked.

Ask lots of questions. There's no need to be a Nosey Parker, but asking lots of general questions will accomplish a few very important things. First of all, it will let you direct conversation to the greatest extent pos-sible. Second of all, it will help you get to know them. Third of all, it will help prevent them from getting to know the real you. If you find yourself short for questions, nothing does the trick like asking to hear some funny (read: embarrassing) stories about your partner, especially stories from their childhood or formative years. If there's one thing I learned growing up with my folks, it's that parents *love* humiliating their kids whenever they get the chance. Take this time with their par-ents as an opportunity to get as much dirt on your partner as possible. If you're really lucky, you'll get to see some photos or old family videos of them, which I can also say from personal experience, is the height of humiliation but ultimately kind of cute.

And, last but not least, the most important thing of all when it comes to meeting the parents:

Courtesy flushing. Absolutely *nothing* is worse than visiting your partner's rents and finding yourself stuck in their bathroom with the toilet clogged and no plunger in sight. It's beyond me why some people still don't leave plungers in their guest bathrooms, but it nonetheless

---

9 The worst is sexual humor. I can't begin to describe how uncomfortable it is when parents you've just met make really nasty sex jokes, or just generally say anything having to do with sex. Goddamn is it disgusting.

remains one of life's many sad facts. So be careful, and remember to flush generously.

If you follow these general guidelines, meeting the parents shouldn't be nearly as dreadful as it is normally. The trick is to always be prepared for anything.

Moving In

At some point in the course of your relationship, you're going to find yourself wanting to live with your partner, either out of simple convenience, or more likely, so you can be around them more often and as much as possible. There are many good reasons to move in, economic and otherwise, but the most important reason is that you simply *want* to live together. Your readiness for something like this will likely vary depending on age, number of past relationships, whether or not you've moved in with someone before, etc. For some people it's an easy transition, and for others it takes some work. In really bad cases, there's no other way to describe it than a fucking nightmare. But you won't know until you try, will you?

Normally, there are two ways of moving in together. One way is for one partner to move into the other's place. The second way is to find a new place together. I recommend the latter, and here's why: one partner moving into the other's place is can put undue stress on both parties involved. One partner has to get used to their space not being theirs exclusively any longer, and the other has to adjust to the feeling as though they're just living in someone else's home. The point of moving in together is to have a home belonging to the *couple*.[10]

When you look for a place together, budget can be a big factor. That said, there are two important factors to be considered:

---

10 If you're on a lease, this could be a pain in the ass. Worse yet if they're on a lease too, and your leases end on different dates. You'll need to work out the logistics. If you're moving into a place together, I wouldn't try living together in one or the other's apartment until the lease is up in the meantime, as this could be a recipe for unmitigated disaster.

Signs things are getting serious

1. They want to have sex with you more than once.

2. Part of your birthday or other holiday presents include homemade "Good for One Free Back Rub" tickets.

3. You don't ever fight with each other.

4. You fight with each other all the time.

5. You've been together longer than you've been together with anyone else.

6. You have pets together.

7. You've met their parents (this only counts if you didn't know their parents before you got together).

8. Your respective family members start putting the pressure on both of you a little more than usual to bear them grandchildren.

9. They playfully slap your ass when you get up to go do the dishes after they finish eating the dinner you cooked for them, and call you "Babe" while doing it.

10. They talk about marriage, kids, moving in together, or going to see any films by Darren Aronofsky.

Space. Some people do fine in small spaces. However, that's normally when they're living by themselves. You're new place doesn't need to be huge (and probably won't be if you're renting, and live on a meager budget like yours truly), but it should allow the both of you enough space so you aren't necessarily spending one hundred percent of your time together in close quarters. It may not seem like it at the moment, but space can be a beneficial thing. You may want some down time on your own to do whatever it is you do (write, draw, paint, music, reading, etc.). Even the best couples can go insane if the individual partners don't have some personal space now and again. Little problems or disagreements can take on exacerbated, larger-than-life dimensions they might not otherwise. A little space can go a long way.

Finances. The thought may have never crossed your mind before, but you should consider how finances are going to be split—or not. That is, will they be divided in some way, equally, or pooled? Speaking from experience, I'm a big fan of pooling, or more explicitly, not a big fan of dividing them. Regardless of what you decide, work out a financial plan together. I know it's not terribly romantic, but money issues aren't something you'll want to encounter farther down the road, and the best way to avoid that is by planning ahead. I'm not saying you've got to al-lot where ever penny of income is going to go, but basic things—bills, rent, and the like—should be discussed and decided on as soon as pos-sible. Unfortunately, one of the biggest stresses and problem-causers for couples is money. If you've got a strong relationship, you're probably not going to let money come between you and your partner. But this doesn't mean it won't ever be an issue, so plan accordingly.

Once you've ironed out how much space you need and how your finances, joint or otherwise, are going to work, start looking online and in newspapers. You'll find something eventually, and perhaps even faster than you imagined. Here's one other thing to consider about housing: do you want to rent or buy? If you're young, like me, buying a house can seem like a *huge* commitment, but if you're in a truly com-mitted relationship, it's no bigger than the one you've already made. While owning a house is nice in principle, the best reason to at least *consider* buying is financial. True, it's a little more expensive initially than renting, but all that money you spend on rent? You're just pissing it away. At least if you buy a place, the payments you make on it (which may not actually cost much more than renting a place) are going to-wards your eventual *ownership* of a home. Also, real estate is a great way to hedge your bets when markets are as uncertain as they are at the moment.

When you've finally found a place, the most important thing is that you make it your own, and when I say "your own," I don't mean yours personally, but yours *as a couple.* This means things as simple as deco-rating it together with relatively equal parts both of your belongings (your Alf doll collection, their S&M gear), breaking in/christening[11] all the rooms[12], or picking out furniture together.[13]

If you can furnish the whole place together good for you. If not, doing it on the cheap ain't so bad. Try flea markets. Usually the best finds can be acquired there. Otherwise, check your local paper's "free" section, as well as announcements about garage and yard sales. It may not always be the nicest or classiest stuff—although on occasion it is—but furniture and decorations you pick up at stuff like this tends to have what my mom would call "a lot of character." In her case, that's a bad thing, but for our purposes here, it's not only great, but things possessing "a lot of character" can be extremely inexpensive.

Living Together

Living together with someone else can be a big change, especially if it's not something you've done before outside the family or friendly setting. It's different than just having housemates, or a roommate. In some respects it's easy as cake, while others can take some adjusting. For instance, being around each other without wanting to go for the throat should be easy. If it's not easy, you may want to reconsider the whole "living together" thing entirely. But, as time passes, you may find things about your partner you hadn't noticed before. Little things. Little things you find unnervingly irritating.

Do they leave the cap off the toothpaste bottle? Do they invariably end up with all the sheets at night or push you off the bed in their sleep? Are they chronically messy? Do they seem to have trouble accomplishing even the most basic daily tasks? Do they have a ridiculously lame sense of humor? What I'm asking is, are they like me? Because if they are, you're going to have your hands full.

---

11 Wink wink, nudge nudge.

12 And counter space. And floors. Oh, and don't forget the shower!

13 Like their S&M torture rack.

Remember what I wrote before about "the whole package" and how when you accept and love someone, that's what you're getting? Well, this is kind of what I was talking about. There are going to be a few things—if not a virtual cornucopia of things—your partner does that will drive you up the fucking wall. But the important thing to keep in mind is it's the same for them. Whether or not you realize it, there are little quirks you have too that might make your partner a bit crazy. In some cases, both of you will have to reform certain behaviors to the greatest extent possible. But in most cases, you'll just need to learn to love it. Because if you really love your partner, you should love their foibles too. They wouldn't be the person they are without them, right?

Aside from this stuff, no matter what anyone else says, living together is pretty damn easy, and *really* nice. Aside from all the (hopefully) great sex, you'll be glad to know there are other benefits too. For one, you don't have to do all the housework yourself, unless you have some kind of "arrangement," by which I mean you're someone's bitch. Split the housework. It creates less stress for both of you, and if you do it together, you might make chores tolerable or even fun. Also, you've got someone to do stuff with. You're not just bored by yourself all the time. Watching movies, going for walks, reading books—all of these things suddenly take on a new light when you're doing them with the person you love more than anything in the entire world. And cooking together? Well, with another vegan, you'll not only eat twice as much[14], but have the joy of cooking for two. Cooking for yourself can be boring and tedious. Cooking with/for someone else is one of the most relaxing things I can think of.

Unless, of course, they're not vegan. Welcome to hell.

If there's one thought I can't stand, it's the thought of having animal shit[15] in my refrigerator. Having to look at it whenever I open the door, smell it, or have the taste of it in any way contaminate my food is a nightmare and a half. It's possible it's just me, but I also loathe

---

14 Don't worry, you'll be having lots and lots of sex to work it all off.

15 Er, products.

the thought of someone cooking meat, dairy, or eggs in my pots and pans. The nice thing about "my" pots and pans and "my" refrigerator, however, are that they are just that—mine. When you're living with someone, almost nothing is "mine." Rather, it's all *ours*.

For some of you, this may not be a big deal. I suspect that more than a few readers could probably tolerate the presence of dairy, and maybe even eggs, in their fridge. You—if you are one of these people—may not mind the stuff being cooked in your pans with your cutlery, either. But I don't think I've ever met a vegan who would play host to rotting animal flesh. Still, I'm sure some of you exist. If you're a vegan living long-term with an omni, this is something you have to deal with on a day-to-day basis, and I suspect you've probably become desensitized to it all. That, or your one of those health food vegans[16] not really into the ethical aspects of your diet/lifestyle. If you can deal with this, then I guess you don't need my advice, and may as well skip ahead to the next section. If not, keep reading. After all, it's not like you're paying for my time or rugged good looks.

If you're a vegan who's fallen for an omni, and is now in a long-term relationship with one, my gut instinct is to first offer you my deepest condolences before we continue. With that out of the way, here are some problems you might run into and how I would suggest you navigate them.

Respect. Sounds like we've covered this one before? Sort of. Here I mean respect in a more specific way. In this case, you're partner needs to respect that you're vegan. If you've been with them for a long time, then they probably already do. In an ideal world, they should also respect that their diet and lifestyle is morally inferior, and not pester you with question, comments, or leaving nasty animal products laying about the icebox. Then again, in an ideal world, they'd probably be vegan in the first place, and all this stuff wouldn't be an issue. So, your partner has to respect you and your veganism. If they make chiding jokes about it, harass you to drop your ethical diet or "cheat" on it,

---

16 Yuck.

try to slip animal product into your food as a "joke," or otherwise act in a fundamentally *dis*respectful manner, it's your job to be firm. Tell them you don't find it acceptable, and won't tolerate it. Period. If this doesn't work then, as my friends Bob and Jenna suggest,[17] it may be a sign of fundamentally deeper problems in the relationship. Also, if you've been together for very long at all, this shouldn't be going on to begin with.

Respect is, however, a two way street. If your partner is a veggie or an omni, you've got to deal with their diet and lifestyle. As much as it would be nice, you can't make them change. This isn't to say you shouldn't hold onto hope that they will, but that you need to respect their choices in the meantime. This is where things can get a little trickier, which we'll delve into now.

Hot, nasty sex? There is probably no greater turn-off, at least in theory, than getting down and dirty with an omni. In most cases, it isn't the simple fact of their diet that's the turn-off, it's the thought of making out with them after a meal, for instance, and ending up with that odd bit of animal matter in your mouth. As I've written elsewhere, love means never having to say "Can you brush your teeth first?"[18] The bitch of it is, you might need to say it anyway, depending on how you feel about a) your partner, and b) their having just consumed a Philly cheesesteak. As you've already decided to commit to a long-term relationship with an omni, I'm not sure a) how much advice I can offer, and b) how valuable it would be anyway. Unfortunately, you'll need to figure out how to deal with this on a case-by-case basis. But if you aren't in an LTR yet, but you would consider one with an omni, this is one more thing you'll have to think about. What if they never decide to go vegan?

---

17 See their amazingly excellent book, *Vegan Freak: Being Vegan in a Non-Vegan World*, Tofu Hound Press, 2005. Or, go to veganfreak.com for more information.

18 See http://www.veganfreak.com/index.php?s=advice

It's not just making out, either. After all, I did title this subsection "hot, nasty sex." Why would sex be an issue? Well, not so much in the act itself, but rather the tools of the trade. Condoms, birth control pills, and S&M gear—if you're into that—typically aren't vegan. All but a couple of condom brands, such as Condomi, Glyde, and Lifestyles contain milk by-products (I have no idea why and was too lazy to do the research), most birth control pills (as well as many other pharmaceuticals) contain lactose, and most S&M gear is, well, leather. You've got to figure out how important it is to you to have vegan condoms, which for most people in the U.S., can't just be picked up at the drugstore.[19] And you have to determine how comfortable you are with having some milk product in your hoo-ha or on your schlong. As is the case with birth control pills, I'd say that an STD or unwanted pregnancy is worse than using a non-vegan contraceptive where no vegan ones are readily available.[20]

As for S&M or BDSM or whatever-you-want-to-call-it gear, you can purchase vegan alternatives online[21] at veganerotica.com or a variety of other sites (here's where google comes in handy). However, for some people, this stuff is just not the same as its leather counterparts. Unlike condoms and birth control pills, however, I don't see this as a valid reason to continue using leather. Pain can be pleasure, but unlike your partner, the cow whose hide you're using didn't consent.

General ideology and other animal rights stuff. It's late one night and you're watching some Frontline special on TV about "animal rights extremists strike again!" As the camera surveys the burned out meat trucks or wrecked vivisection lab, you notice your boy/girl/whatever-friend isn't quite cheering on the most recent Animal Liberation Front

---

19 For instance, cellophane/Saran/plastic wrap is not a valid vegan substitute for a condom, nor is aluminum foil, nor is that really neat new Glad wrap with the little air bubbles that makes it seal to any surface(!)

20 I probably should have also mentioned in the main body of the text that not all sex toys and lubes are vegan either. You can find vegan alternatives to all these and more in the wondrous world of the internet—or, as our remedial fuckwit cokehead of a president says, "the Internets."

21 For more information, consult Bob and Jenna's book, *Vegan Freak*, as footnoted above.

hit like you. In fact, they may look downright uneasy. It's at this point you realize your omni partner may not be totally down with your whole "AR" gig. If you're with an omni, it's probably tolerable because even if they aren't vegan, they're at least an animal *lover*, right? No, not in the freak-nasty Catherine the Great sense, but they're probably one of those hipster fuckheads that not only likes your pets, they try to eat organic, "free range" dead animals. But deep down inside, they either think you're taking love of animals too far, or feel like you're doing something they'd never be capable of. Note that if it's the latter, your love, patience, and guidance can make a great vegan out of them some day, so long as you don't fuck it all up. But if its the former, you should dump the [insert appropriate gender pronoun/expletive here] to the curb. If your partner thinks—again, deep down—that you're a fucking loony, it's probably best you not waste your time, vegan culinary skills, and striking good looks on their sorry omni ass.

Pets

One great way to bond with your partner and form a cohesive family sans children is through companion animals. If you don't already have any, there are an abundance of lonesome animals out there that need adoption. Far too many, in fact. Whatever your position on pet ownership—i.e., whether or not you view the notion of "owning" an animal extremely distasteful, or whether you don't really feel one way or the other about it—nothing changes this fact. Even if you and your partner live in a place with a "no pets" policy, these rules generally refer to large animals like cats, dogs, and other animals that roam free around your apartment and hence may cause damage. Even then, if you offer to put down a security deposit, or a larger one than you are already putting down, some places will make exceptions. Also, oftentimes small animals that typically live in cages will be exempt from such policies. This includes guinea pigs, rabbits, mice, gerbils, rats, etc. For instance, I've never had a problem with my rats, even in apartments with fairly stringent "no pets" rules. Plus, it's easy enough to sneak in small animals like this. Today, my partner and I have four lovely female rats and one equally lovely, albeit larger, female cat, all adopted.

If I haven't done so already, let me stress the adoption aspect of pet ownership. I used to own a dog my girlfriend (at the time) and I purchased from a breeder as a puppy. In retrospect, this was incomprehensible moral negligence on my part. Granted, we didn't get her from a puppy mill (more on this momentarily) but with all of the animals out there in need of good homes, it is just plain wrong to help any industry, even small breeding operations, that bring new pets into a world already unable to deal with those already in existence.

When you walk by a pet store in the mall—one that sells live animals, as opposed to the kind that only sell pet supplies—what you see inside are puppies, kittens, and other animals bred in mills. Puppy mills are basically like factory farms, except instead of producing eggs or dairy, they produce puppies. Breeder females are impregnated over and over again until they are no longer "productive," and are then killed. The puppies are born into miserable conditions, and as much as up to *half* die before arriving at your local pet store.[22] When you buy a milled animal, you are directly supporting this brutal industry, and simultaneously denying the hundreds of thousands of animals already out there for adoption a home, many of whom are on death row at kill shelters. Please, if you actually take any one piece of advice from this book, *adopt.*

Adopting an animal together is a big endeavor, and while certainly fun, not to be taken lightly. This animal is depending on you and your partner for the rest of its natural life. If you aren't sure, or are only "kind of sure" you'd like a pet, *don't get one.* If, however, the two of you have thought it through extensively, it can be one of the greatest decisions you will ever make. Companion animals have the ability to enrich your life in ways you may have never dreamed possible, as you will undoubtedly enrich theirs.

---

22 See Gary Francione's *Introduction to Animal Rights: Your Child or the Dog?* for more information.

Engagement

Much like the phrase "long-term relationships," the very word "engage-ment" or "engaged" strikes fear into the heart of noncommittal men and women the country over. But, as with LTRs, you needn't much worry. Honestly, speaking from personal experience I never imagined I'd be engaged. I "wanted to be some day," but figured it was like how I wanted to be a fireman or an astronaut when I was but a wee boy.

Without getting all gushy, one of the things I have to credit my part-ner, Jenna, with is helping me realize that when there's something you know you want, sometimes the only way to get it is to just do it; do what you know makes you happy, and fuck all else. So I asked her to marry me. Really, this is my advice to all of you: do what makes you happy; fuck all else. You *know* what makes you happy. So at the risk of sounding like a two dollar bumper sticker, why waste a minute of your life doing anything else?

If you're young-ish like myself[23], and considering getting engaged to your partner, I suspect most of your anxieties about any potential engagement have to do not with the person you want to marry, but your concerns about how others will react. Remember the whole "fuck all else" thing I just wrote about? Well, that includes people. So fuck everyone else. No, not literally. My point is that you can't spend your whole life pleasing other people and living exactly the way they ex-pect of you. If you know what will make you happy—and not just now, but *very* long term, like *forever*—is to spend the rest of your life with your partner and no one else, then why waste time on worrying what other people will think? Your friends will probably support you as friends are supposed to do, and everyone else will come around in time. In the meantime, you'll likely hear things like, "You're too young to be engaged," or, "You're too young to know what you really want," or, "You're young, you don't really want to be tied down, this is when you're supposed to be free and having all sorts of new experiences."

---

23 Hell, even if you're not. It's just that older people tend not to frown as much on their peers becoming engaged.

There are a number of problems with all of these statements, which either base maturity solely on age or imply that marriage is something older people are simply relegated too after their good years have passed them by. But more importantly, all of this is simply meaningless tripe and banter coming from younger people your age who are themselves commitmentphobes, or older people who don't know it's not their own marriage they're dissatisfied with, but rather themselves. In both cases, it's just other cynical people putting their own insecurities, shortcomings, and failures (or fear of failure) onto you. Not only is this grossly unfair, most of it's not worth listening to. In the end, they just want you to be as miserable as they are. Don't buy into their bullshit. Keep your eye on what makes you happy, what brings you joy, and you'll be fine.

This isn't necessarily to say that your friends won't have some legitimate reservations. But you'll know these for what they are when you get them, as they'll likely be conveyed in a rational, well-reasoned, or concerned manner, and not as bitter, cynical, or vindictive. That is, so long as your friends aren't all bitter, cynical, vindictive assholes. If that's the case, you just need to find new friends. If any of your friends approach you in this way, it means that they'll actually be open to you assuaging their concerns, and gaining their total and unreserved support.

Oh, a word on rings. As a point of practical advice, if you're going to get your partner an engagement ring, or if you're both going to wear rings, for the love of God, don't buy diamonds. Most of these come from conflict zones, and even so-called "conflict-free" diamonds are nearly impossible to verify as such, no matter what any jeweler tells you. As a vegan, purchasing analogs should be nothing new to you, so stick to imitations, or just go with a simple band, unless you happen to have a diamond ring that's a family heirloom of some sort and you don't feel weird about the invariable amount of suffering contained in the bling bling itself.

Gettin' Hitched

To cover the intricacies and complexities of marriage would require a book in and of itself, as well as a degree I do not possess, so I'm just going to go over some brief logistical things pertaining to the actual ceremony itself. You may get a lot of pressure from relatives to do things their way, and it might be hard to say no if they're providing any sort of financial support for the ceremony, let alone the bulk of it. If this happens, you've got two choices: do things their way, or do the wedding on the cheap. The extreme cheap. If you opt for the latter, as I would if given the two options, you'll be faced with another potential problem: your relatives may *really* not like that. Hopefully, this will force them into some concessions. Ultimately, the point is not to make too many compromises. Some are probably inevitable, but they needn't all be. Remember, it's *your* wedding.

Wedding dresses are fucking expensive. I guess I knew this already, but I'd never shopped around for them until recently. Not for myself, of course; I'm not planning on wearing a dress—this would probably be too much for my folks to handle. But after looking in a bridal shop with my partner, we noticed that not only are the dresses *really* expensive, many of them are also *really* not vegan. That is to say, they are made of/with silk, pearls, and a few items even had fur trim—shit, they might as well have been made of fucking veal smothered in cream sauce. This sort of leaves us, and probably you, with two options: a less expensive simple cotton dress, or a more expensive synthetic dress. I suspect we'll opt for the cotton.[24]

It being a vegan wedding and all (assuming both of you are vegan), the big challenge, and likely your biggest expense, will be catering. If it's a relatively small wedding, the challenge might not be so daunting. If you have as many relatives as, say, Jenna, catering is going to be a downright bitch. As we're not married yet, and won't be for some time due to financial constrictions (we're both paupers), I'm not sure how

---

24 Jenna Torres tells me that many non-silk satin or poly-blend wedding dresses with beads or sequins are actually cheaper than their silk/pearl counterparts. As she's actually been through the whole wedding process, I trust her on this one.

we're going to pay for it. But the more important task in your case, as well as ours, is finding a vegan caterer.

Now I'm not saying the caterer needs to be *exclusively* vegan in all their dealings, although this would be ideal, but they need to at least know what "vegan" means. Oddly enough, some don't. As it requires a lot of work and extremely careful label reading on their part, more than a few catering companies will simply refuse to even make vegan meals unless they are dead simple. Considering it's your wedding, you'll probably want to serve more than pasta with red sauce or grilled vegetables. And frankly, as far as the financial breakdown of a wedding goes, food is where I'm willing to drop the most money.

Also, you'll have to decide if you're only going to offer a vegan option. To me, at least, this is a no-brainer: there's no way in fuck I'm going to have a single bit of animal product served at my wedding. While the decision may in theory be easy, however, it's possible it may upset some relatives. For instance, I'm told by a trusted source[25] that Jenna has a lot of vegetarian relatives, and most of the rest are at least veggie-friendly. Unfortunately, I'm not as sure my family—extended family, at least—would be quite so forgiving of a vegan-only meal. Then again, it ain't their wedding, is it? I urge you to make your wedding cruelty-free and only offer vegan menu options. Your relatives, no matter how meat-obsessed, will just have to deal. Also, if you have a good caterer, you may even turn a few on to vegan food, which can't hurt.

Then again, if you're marrying an omni, they will probably want a non-vegan menu option; perhaps even more than one. Maybe it's just me, but I would have a hard time celebrating my love of someone else in the presence of a hundred people all chowing on dead animal flesh. And that's how I'd put it to your omni bride/huband-to-be when patiently explaining they don't really have a choice in the matter. But, if you're a pushover, chances are you'll concede to their complaints and

---

25 Jenna

incessant whining.[26] Again, the credo to remember about your marriage ceremony is, *it's* your *wedding.*

It should be noted that some places actually host specifically vegan weddings, including catering, etc. In my home state, there's the Sweet Onion Inn, a vegan bed and breakfast in the countryside. Unfortunately for my partner and me, they put a cap on weddings of forty people, which is the minimum number of relatives I'm told to expect from her side alone. But such places exist, and if you can afford one, I'd take your business there as it's always better to support the vegan-run alternative of anything when and where it exists.

Vegan, Veggie, Omni: What's the Difference?
Mixed marriages, mixed refrigerators

Living with and/or being married to another vegan can be remarkably easy in the sense that it's unlike living with an omni or even a vegetarian. You don't have to worry about a pile of frozen meat in an oversized zip-lock bag greeting you when you go to get ice, you don't have to feel self-conscious about yourself when going off on a rant about animal rights, and best of all, you don't need to explain your philosophical and ethical leanings as they pertain to *everything.* Because these things can get tiring. They're easier than other relationships in the sense that you only need to worry about normal relationship stuff, and not "the vegan thing" and "the omni thing." They can be *better* than other relationships in that a strong ethical life practice and outlook like veganism can bring the two partners in the relationship closer together, strengthening their bond. And they can be *worse* than other relationships because if things start to go wrong—and here I mean really, really, irreparably wrong—you can become reluctant to end them. Not only does it take a long-ass time to meet someone else, get to know them, and get through all the usual bullshit, there's also the added aspect that at least the person you're with now, as shitty as they might be, is vegan.

---

26 Omnis tend to whine a lot. I don't know why. Really, I think it's because they're just little bitches at heart.

And that makes the already tall order of a functional relationship even taller. Whether they end up being worse, the same, or better than other relationships is largely up to and based on the couple itself.

Living with and/or being married to an omni can also, no doubt, be easy as well. For instance, you needn't deal twenty-four hours a day with some annoying-ass vegan, as many vegans are, from my experience, *really fucking annoying*. They're better because... well, they're not better than a relationship with a vegan. But they could probably be about the same. Oh, and they can *definitely* be worse, although I'm unsure I really need to go into the specifics here. I'm sure your imagination will suffice. But hey, you love them, right? And that's all that matters.[27]

Living with and/or being married to a veggie can be easy in the sense that they might become a vegan, and at least you don't have to deal with all that meat lying around. Of course, there is the possibility for an omni to go vegan, don't get me wrong. Most of us aren't born vegan. You just have to find a comfortable strategy to help them make the jump. Anyway, same thing with veggies. Let's be honest. While a relationship with a veggie might be better than one with an omni, it probably won't be as rewarding as one you'd have with a vegan. What makes it *worse* than other relationships is they'll be hypersensitive in a way that not even omnis are about you making moral judgments of them. If you want the relationship to be happy, make sure they know you're not judging them.[28]

The Vegan Mentor

There's a good chance your partner will become vegan. It's not always a great chance, but there's nearly always one present. This is where you need to be a vegan mentor. Being a vegan mentor is a bit like being

---

27 Oh, come on, you just knew there was going to be a footnote for that, right? Seriously, maybe that's all that matters to you. But long term, I could not be with an omni if they didn't eventually become vegan. Doesn't mean you can't do it. Hell, you can do whatever you want. Ain't my funeral.

28 Even if you are, in fact, judging the fuck out of them.

Obiwan in Star Wars, winning folks to the light side, the Vegan Order, and training them in the ways of the Soya, except without all the cool shit. Oh, and there's no Vegan Academy on Couresant. Or lightsabres—sorry, kids. But you do get that sweet-ass hooded robe. Okay, no, you don't. Actually, you get a copy of John Robbins's *Diet for a New America* and a cookbook. But really, this is all it should take.

Every vegetarian-turned-vegan had their own vegan mentor, whether they'd admit to it or not. In my case, it was a bit more removed, in the form of vegan-related music. However, with other people, it's normally, well, other people. In this shortish subsection, I'm going to provide a few tips on how you too can be a goodly vegan mentor.

Traditionally speaking, there are two ways of making more vegans. One is the fun way,[29] but involves paying for the little fuckers' college educations at some point. The other way is mentoring veggies, and in some cases omnis. When approaching them about veganism, here's some shit to keep in mind:

1. *Don't approach vegetarians or omnis about veganism.* It will just make them feel pressured.

Okay, so that was really the only tip I had about approaching them. But once *they've* approached *you* about veganism (in any capacity), here're my suggestions:

1. *Let them ask whatever questions they like, no matter how trite or asinine, and answer them honestly, no matter how much the truth hurts.* This means when someone asks, "As a vegan, will I have to be involved in the ritual sacrifice of human babies?" you've got an obligation to say, "Yes, and it will need to be your first born." Alternately, if someone just asks, "So, what *do* you eat?" which is a slightly easier question, you're also going to need to tell them the truth—"Your first born. Or, you know, tofu." These conversations can often occur during meals. This is a good time to invite them to try some of whatever you're eating. If you hear

objections like, "Um, that's okay, I'm fine with this cheese pizza," be firm: "Look, I don't care if it is your first born, you're being a goddamned sissy." Or, if you're eating tofu, explain it's not all that bad. While few omnis dabble in tofu cookery, many vegetarians have likely have, and most of them have only made it once. Know why? Because they fucked it up the first time, or just ate plain, raw, silken tofu (shudder). You're job under these circumstances is to show them vegan food is yummers, even if they are a big sissy.

2. *Never give them shit about eating dairy, eggs, honey, etc.* I guess with omnis, this goes for meat too, as hard as that is. Ultimately, this won't be productive. Instead, I suggest dosing their animal product food with small amounts of arsenic. This way they can easily be weaned off of them. Of course, the arsenic in small doses will eventually become addictive, and you'll need to continue upping the amount which will at some point kill them, but are you interested in saving animals or not? Or, if you're a big sissy too, you should avoid giving them shit because it will make them uneasy about approaching you. The key to winning people over is being approachable. If you can't be approachable about veganism, then you might as well not be vegan at all, because you're doing squat to aid the greater cause. The golden rule here: be patient, give gentle reminders.

3. *Don't make inordinate promises about the benefits of veganism.* It's fine to tell your padwan learner veganism is healthier than vegetarianism, more ethically consistent, and not a difficult switch to make. But don't make promises you can't keep. Attention vegetarians/omnis: no matter what anyone tells you, becoming vegan will not make you part of an international crime syndicate, "the family," the "tofu nostra," or the vegan mob; that is, not unless you really want to get involved with PeTA.

4. *Your library is their library.* Give your unwitting pupil lots of books, literature, and videos about veganism and AR issues.

Don't frame it as something they have to examine, rather, just extend the offer. You'll be surprised by how frequently people take you up on it.

5. *When they are ready, help them to construct their first lightsabre as they prepare to strike down their own father in a blaze of well-choreographed swordplay.* Fuck, we *totally* need lightsabres.

6. *If you know other vegans, hang out together with your veggie/omni partner.* Show them other vegans are out there too, and they're not all as weird as you. Demonstrating a broader base of support will make your true love feel more encouraged. The three B's—Bowling, BBQ, and Bloody child sacrifice—are all great ways to make your "student" feel more welcome in the world of veganism.

7. *Don't give them too much too fast.* Too much information too fast can break vegetarians and turn omnis off completely. Their minds are fragile, and you'll do well to remember this.

8. *Once they make the leap, they'll need support.* Think of yourself as the training wheels for your new vegan apprentice. Some day they will graduate to a real bike, but not yet. The important thing is to help them to not "cheat." Sometimes new vegans are prone to do this, and while it's not a great sign, it's also not a death sentence on their veganism. In fact, the more you verbally tell them you don't care if they cheat, the more guilt they'll feel. In this case, that's probably okay. The important thing they must realize is that they aren't "cheating" animals, they're only cheating themselves. Also, new vegans will eat a host of non-vegan things without knowing it. This can result in a lot of guilt, shame, or embarrassment when you point out that, say, the soy cheese they purchased with the best of intentions contains casein. Reassure them they haven't done anything wrong, and remind them veganism isn't about purity and perfection, it's about doing your best. Most of all, it's a learning process. Even seasoned (no pun intended) vegan veterans make mistakes from time to time–sometimes big

ones. While there's virtually no way around this, it doesn't make veganism pointless, and it's important to remind your learner of this point.

If you follow these steps, you'll have a vegan in no time. Actually, that's a lie. It can frequently take years for someone to finally become vegan. But if you're patient, *you can get them there.* Just be encouraging, supportive, loving, and patient. In time, they may even give up their child willingly.[30]

And if all else fails, sit down with your partner, a bowl of popcorn, some of those little airline vomit bags, and a copy of the documentary *Earthlings*. This is the atomic bomb of the vegan arsenal, so try to exhaust all other possibilities first. If they still show no signs of moving towards veganism, there's little more advice I can proffer. As with everything else in veganism, you'll need to decide your own limits.

A Concluding Word of Consolation

So that's the skinny on the much-dreaded LTR. I'm not sure there's much else I can offer here except good luck and best wishes. Keep plugging away; even if you don't catch on to everything immediately, it will all come with time. And if you're stuck with an omni you really do love, don't worry about all the trash talking on my part. Some omnis are genuinely good people, they're just dietarily confused. Even if you can't help them sort out the confusion, it doesn't mean you can't have a long, loving relationship with them. And if you can, you're a better person than I. Then again, most of you are already probably better people than I could ever hope to be, so maybe that's not such a leap. But my point is, there are no barriers to love, even veganism.

---

30 In the case of your partner, this will likely assume the form of the book-turned-movie, Rosemary's Baby.

chapter **5**

The Sex Chapter, or, Everything You Ever Wanted to Know About Vegan Sex but Were Afraid to Ask

You really must have seen this chapter coming, even if you didn't read the table of contents. After all, what's left to cover except steamy, raunchy, messy, vegan sex? This chapter is also why I almost didn't publish under my real name.[1] Come on, you think I need my parents reading this? Aside from the fact they aren't vegan, even if they did read it I wouldn't want to know, and I certainly wouldn't want them to know I wrote it. So before I start thinking in the "parents and my sex chapter" vein too deeply, let's just continue with the damned chapter introduction, okay?

---

1   As you may have noticed, I did publish under my real name. But don't think my parents even know this book exists. I just hope to high heaven they don't find it on Amazon or some shit.

While regular, everyday omni sex has its ethical implications to be sure, vegan sex has more of them, as we'll soon see. In this chapter, we'll cover among other things safe sex, sex toys, the seemingly elusive female orgasm, cunnilingus, anal play, birth control and condoms, the ethics of things like BDSM and abortion as they relate to veganism, keeping things interesting in the bedroom, and that age old question, "So, are blowjobs vegan?"

Safe Sex

Honestly, it's not that I want to rehash your middle school, high school, or whatever year's worth of classes about safe sex. Then again, if you lived in the south, maybe you didn't have classes like this, so who knows. Or, maybe you just got the "abstinence only" education, in which case you're probably a bit overdue for the whole sex talk, aren't you? Or, maybe you were home schooled.[2] Hey, how the fuck should I know?

Playing safe is important, you know, if you're going to... you know. If you're still just dating or fucking about, *use a goddamned condom, will you?* This goes for guys and girls alike, but mostly guys. Fellas, listen: I know you think that "it just doesn't feel the same," or whatever, but you know what else doesn't feel the same? Living with genital warts, HIV, syphilis, gonorrhea, crabs, and any other fun variety of STDs.[3] And you never know when the next outbreak of the ebola virus is going to happen (although until now its major outbreaks have all occurred in African countries, so maybe that's only a concern if you live somewhere on the African continent, or just happen to be traveling there while you read this). So wrap it up.

---

2 Ha!

3 I'm told the proper term as of the past couple of years is "STIs," or, "Sexually Transmitted Infections" (as opposed to "Sexually Transmitted Diseases") because the word "disease" was too stigmatizing. I don't know, call me old fashioned, but perhaps the disease itself should be a stigma if that will help people protect themselves from getting it—whatever "it" is. Don't get me wrong, I'm not saying people with STDs should be stigmatized, as they often are, but if it's just "an infection," how does that make people want to play it safer? I don't think it does.

And while wrapping, you should know that a variety of things you may have learned, as I did, in your secondary school Sex Ed classes are, in fact, wrong. Most notably, don't double-bag it. For those of you unfamiliar with sex slang, this means *don't wear two condoms at once.* When I was but a youngin', we were told that two were better than one: in case one broke, the other would still be there under it. In reality, this significantly increases the likelihood that *both* condoms will break due to the friction of the two against each other. Trust me on this one, one condom is enough. And if you're a gay male or one of the many (and there are lots of them) straight couples having a whole lot of butt sex, *use lube* even if the condom is already lubricated in some way. Not only should this make things a whole lot more comfortable for your partner, it also decreases the chances of your condom breaking, so long as you use actual lube and not shit like vaseline, which will actually corrode the latex. It should be noted that certain lubes, especially silicone-based brands, will also erode latex. For vegan lubricants, see VeganErotica online.

It can be hard to make putting a condom on "sexy" if you're a guy, and the last thing you want to do is go limp as a wet noodle while still struggling to open the damn condom box, tear one off, then open *that one* up as well, figure out which end is up, and roll it on, all in front of someone you haven't had sex with before, or at least not much of it. This is when it's important to have a sense of humor. If you take sex too seriously, you'll only succeed in performing poorly even if you manage to get your under-the-belt raincoat on. Sex is supposed to be fun, and at times, fun*ny*. Oh, and guys? Don't open the condom wrapper with your teeth. You may think you're girl/guy will find it hot, but trust me, they'll just be confused; and there's an extremely good chance you'll damage the condom in doing so. Also, watch the finger nails when putting it on. You don't want any holes. Most importantly—and I do know how stupid this sounds—please, please RTFM.[4]

---

4   Read The Fucking Manual. Condom boxes come with instructions—contrary to popular belief—for a reason. You might actually try reading them some time, as obvious as all things dick-related would seem to guys. For instance, did you know

Surprisingly or not, just as most guys seem to have not the faintest idea about vaginas and their inner workings, so too many women just don't get penises. I mean, they know that when rubbed enough they shoot some hot gooey stuff out, but beyond that, they don't get what exactly causes erections, why they can suddenly go away, and the other mechanics of the wonderful world of phalluses. So guys, if you're having problems, tell them. *Explain.* If they're bitchy about it, then show them the door. Because otherwise, there's a decent chance *they're* going to think they are doing something wrong, when nothing could be further from the truth. You know, except for watching you struggle ineptly to pull a simple piece of latex over your junk before they dry up from the sheer boredom of it all. Sorry, I know that last sentence probably didn't help.

Condoms, if you read the box and manual, if used correctly will prevent pregnancy and greatly reduce the risk of contracting an STD. Note the use of the word *reduce.* This doesn't mean if you use a condom you're home free as far as unpleasant "infections" go. Some STDs are still contractable, even with condom use. Genital warts, for instance, is still transmissible even if you're using a condom. The warts themselves are a manifestation of HPV, or Human Papilloma Virus. HPV is itself is an interesting phenomenon, as about fully two thirds of the population has it. This doesn't mean, however, that two thirds of the population has genital warts. Most of the time, HPV will not manifest itself in any outward way whatsoever, and will take no toll on your health or time off your life span. My point is, in the scheme of things—especially compared to other STDs—HPV isn't something you should worry about too much, as there's nothing you can do to prevent from contracting it short of not having sexual contact with anyone, ever.

---

you're supposed to gently pinch the reservoir tip with your thumb and forefinger as you roll the rest of the condom on? I bet you didn't. But you are. I promise you'll learn at least one new thing about condoms if you just read the directions. Girls, this goes for you too. Guys tend to be kind of dumb, and part of that includes a seemingly genetic imperative that we never, ever, read directions. For anything. Ever. Ever. So, in knowing this, you should take it upon yourself to read the directions too. That way, you can embarrass your partner/date in your advanced knowledge of condoms that far eclipses their own.

However, there are still other things you can contract even with condom usage, so as previously stated, RTFM.

For you lesbians out there, condoms probably won't be of as much use to you, with scant exception (for instance, you can put them over dildos or fingers). For you, there is a special treat: the dental dam! This lovely tool of the dental trade can be used for all sorts of oral fun, although as with penis-involved oral sex, I'm not sure how fun mouth-on-latex action is. But the important thing, so far as we are concerned here, is that it's safe.

To be as safe as possible, there are two more things you need to do. One is get tested. There are a variety of clinics in most places that will provide free STD or HIV/AIDS testing. The other is to not feel the need to have sex with every person you meet who's remotely interested (or interesting). It's cliché to be sure, but remember that when you sleep with someone, you're sleeping with everyone they've ever slept with. And everyone that all the people they've slept with have slept with. And—well, you get the point. In the end, that's a lot of people. You know, unless you live in an Amish community or something, in which case you probably don't have nearly as much to worry about. But then again, if you're living in an Amish community, you're probably not reading this are you, you carriage-driving, no-electricity-using, barn-raising, beard-having sonofabitch? No. I didn't think so.

It would be perhaps neglectful of me to point out that the safest sex is no sex. Or, in lieu of no sex, phone sex. Or, in lieu of phone sex, dry humping.

Toys

A bit about toys. Some people really like sex toys. I mean *really* like them. As in, *sex is not fun without them* for these folks. If you're one of them, or you just like a buttplug up your ass once in a while, it's important your toys are cruelty-free. This is where sex-positive sites like VeganErotica.com or Toys in Babeland come in handy, but also where you might try consulting your local sex shop. Most people like ordering online better, as it saves them the embarrassment of walking into a sex shop, and if you're young looking, having to present a photo ID to the clerk in addition to the normal feelings of shame and humiliation. But in this case, the clerk is exactly who you want to talk to. If they're a sex store owner or employee worth their salt, they should know all about most of the products they're selling, including whether or not they are made completely of synthetic stuff, or whether or not they contain any obvious animal products. And that goes for lube too, not just the toys themselves. A lot of lube, just like whatever hand soap or other crap you liked to jerk off with as a teenager, is made with animal products. I think this is not only a really weird notion, but also an incredibly disgusting one (the lube thing that is, not you jerking off, although that might be incredibly disgusting as well. Who's to say?).

Some people are weird about sex toys; they come with some kind of stigma attached to them. Frankly, they've never been my bag and, I suspect, never will be. But, that doesn't mean you shouldn't take some for at least a test drive if, deep down inside, they've piqued your naughty, naughty interest. Toys don't make you some kind of weird pervert (unless that's "your thing"). Plenty of other people use them. After all, with all those sex shops out there and online, someone's buying the stuff. Trust me, they probably beat your removable shower head, vibro-pen, or whatever else you've been using because you're too embarrassed to show your face in a shop.

A Brief Lesson in Female Mechanics, the "Elusive" Female Orgasm, and Cunnilingus for the Cunning Linguist

If you already have a vagina, this section probably won't be of much use to you, unless you are one of the sadly uninformed girls who thinks something is wrong with her because she hasn't reached orgasm to date, with or without a partner. If this sounds familiar, we'll get to you in a moment. Really, this is little bit is intended mostly, although not exclusively, for guys.

So here it is, all you men out there: while the vaginal orgasm isn't a *total* myth, it's *mostly* or *often* a total myth. Most women experience orgasms *only* from direct stimulation of the clitoris. Women who do have so-called "vaginal orgasms" (that is, orgasms induced from internal stimulation from, say, a penis, fingers, fist, vibrator, or Barbie doll) achieve these by stimulation of nerves linked to the clitoris. So really, your cock probably just isn't going to do it, and it doesn't matter how much of a "big man" you are. Don't worry, if you didn't know this it's not because you're an idiot, you just made a false assumption, probably based on watching way too much porn growing up.[5] As I stated a moment ago, there are a surprising number of women who think something is wrong with them because they cannot achieve vaginal orgasm, just like you think something is wrong with you for not being able to help them get there. So let's get something straight: nothing is wrong with either of you.[6] While stimulation of other parts of the female genitalia may feel nice, even *really* nice, if you want to give her the gift of orgasm, it's going to take some tongue or finger work on your part focused on the clitoris—not the labia, not the entrance to the vagina, not inside the vagina. This isn't to say women receive no pleasure at all from having you inside of them; they can receive an immense amount just as you can. But, unlike you, they probably just aren't going to climax that way.

When I was in college, I remember regularly hearing guys in my dorm bitch about giving oral to women, treating it either as a chore, or as downright disgusting. That's why these same guys almost never get laid, can't keep a steady girlfriend, and if they do, their girlfriend is totally dissatisfied inside. If any of them are married today, then their Stepford wives are probably all sleeping with the pool boy, who as underpaid and stupid as he might be, probably at least knows how their plumbing works. Then again, these guys were probably going down on omni girls, who don't always smell quite so nice as their vegan coun-

---

5 Or, you know, yesterday.

6 And if she has been reaching "orgasm" during intercourse, it's likely not real. Sorry, guys. But hey, at least she likes you enough to make you feel special, right?

terparts. The point, however, is that oral isn't a chore, and unless your partner is suffering from a really nasty yeast infection, has their period,[7] or both, shouldn't be revolting to you either.

Oral takes practice. Lots, and lots of practice. *Especially* cunnilingus. I've always found it funny that some women—often married women in groups—actually pay people to *give them lessons* on blowjobs. Don't get me wrong, I'm sure their husbands appreciate it and everything, but men's plumbing is just not very complicated. You rub it enough, and it's going to go off. While good technique is undoubtedly nice, a necessity it's not. The folks who really need "oral lessons" are guys (or lesbians, I guess, but technique probably comes more naturally to them[8]). It's hard to give lessons without visuals, but really the most important things you need remember, and let your mantra be, is "focus on the clit." While this focus doesn't need to exclude other parts of the vagina and body, it should probably constitute at least eighty-five percent of it.[9] And while you're focusing, do remember that the clitoris is far more sensitive than the penis, as it contains a significantly greater number of nerve endings. This means that while it is indeed your focus, don't get rough. Unless they ask, that is.

Of course, a lot of licking isn't all it takes. You've also got to have some skill. If you don't have a lot of experience in the oral department, this is going to take some time and experimentation. Oh, and a girlfriend. You'll need one of those too[10]. And she'll need to be communicative, more on which anon.

---

7   Truthfully, I have heard of some guys who are turned on by this. What the fuck is wrong with you assholes? Not that I'm judging, of course.

8   After a careful review of the manuscript and discussions with friends, I am not sure this statement has any basis in reality. But I left it in the final printing anyway. In fact, I even footnoted it. How d'ya like them apples?

9   While this is a totally arbitrary number, it's a good place to start.

10 Unless you've got the money to learn with a prostitute, although I'm not sure how safe that is, and prostitution is illegal in most states. That said, if you're interested, look up "Escorts" or "Escort Services" in your local yellow pages (as far as I know there

So, Are Blowjobs Vegan?[11]

Yes.[12]

Forbidden Fruit: Anal Play for the Anal Retentive

With the exception of gay men, if there's one thing couples seem to be genuinely afraid of even considering, it's anal play. This can take a variety of forms, ranging from tongues to fingers, plugs[13] to dildos, vibrators to anal beads, strap-ons to cocks. For some folks, it can even take the form of small furry animals; however, being vegan, I hope you can recognize the inherent cruelty with this last possibility. Anyway, the point is, straight people may love a good ass, but have a lot of hang-ups when it comes to doing anything beyond grabbing, slapping, spanking, or periodically biting them (playfully, not in the cannibalistic sense).

Anal play has an unfortunate stigma: assholes are dirty, or they smell bad, or it's "unnatural." People view it as the exclusive domain of gay men, who are sadly still viewed by a great many as being sexual deviants, and Catholic priests, who are sadly still viewed by a great many as not being sexual deviants. Allow me to spell out exactly *why* these stigmas are just so unfortunate. In men, this is where the prostate is located, also known as "the male G-spot." Stimulation of the prostate internally, especially in conjunction with external stimulation of the penis, can produce some serious fireworks. Likewise, I hear the feel-

---

are never listings for "Prostitute," "Hooker," "Whore," "Street Walker," "Woman of the Night," or "Sex Worker").

11 Surprisingly, I get this question a lot when people find out I'm vegan. It usually comes right after some quip about "How do you know plants don't feel pain?"

12 So long as both parties are willing.

13 It's come to my attention that many people don't know what buttplugs are, except that it's a fantastic insult to shout at someone if timed properly. There are a lot of myths about them; that, for instance, they are something for aging gay men who have had too much anal sex, and now wear them all the time to keep the shit from falling straight out their ass. This is obviously (or, I hope obviously) ridiculous. People wear plugs during sex (or sex acts) to provide extra stimulation and intensify orgasm. That's it. Corks they are not.

ing of anal penetration can be extremely enjoyable for women, too. As with men, however, not all women agree.

Like any sexual contact, safety is of the utmost importance. If you're not careful, it's possible to do some unpleasant damage to your partner, or just cause them pain. That's why if you're inserting more than a finger, play it safe and use lube (you may want to use it regardless, just make sure it's vegan). And, like with oral, it's important to communicate with your partner about what feels good and what doesn't. To begin with, unless you're totally comfortable with and trusting of each other, you should talk about anal action before engaging in it. Not all people are the same regarding their sexual proclivities, and not all like having surprises of this particular nature sprung on them whilst in bed.[14] But let me be clear: having anal fun doesn't mean you're perverted, weird—any weirder than you already are, that is—or gay. Just think of it as an additional way of expanding your sexual horizons.

Insecurities

Men and women, guys and girls—all are touched in one way or another by a variety of sexual insecurities, whether it's women with physical insecurities about how their bodies are "supposed to look," whether or not they should be having vaginal orgasms, or how big their breasts are, or guys, who worry about stuff like premature ejaculation and penis size. The bottom line: if you want to have any hope of a normal, happy, healthy sex life, you gotta ditch this shit. It does no good, is usually untrue, and at worst, can be a self-fulfilling prophecy. So let me say, unequivocally: girls, your breasts are not too small. Even if you're flat as a wall, not every guy, contrary to popular belief, wants D cups, or even Bs. You probably aren't even capable of vaginal orgasms. There's no such thing as "too big" an ass. Guys, you don't need a nine inch dick to please women.[15] Not only would that huge cock you so lust

---

14 Or on the couch, countertop, in the shower, public restrooms... you know, wherever it is you like to get it on.

15 If you're curious, the average penis size for men is six inches. The only exception to this are German men, who, according to a study by Condomi, have slightly smaller

after probably just hurt your partner, if you *really* want to please your partner sexually, worry more about your tongue—and not how big it is, but what it can do. Premature ejaculation? It's possible you suffer from it. But it's far more likely whatever issues you're having in that department can be cured through: more sex, more jerking off, or more sex. Did I mention that more sex would help? Because it would. This helps desensitize the penis. Not completely, of course, but enough that sex can last ten or twenty minutes instead of ten or twenty seconds. Also, no matter what Sting says about being able to have sex for hours at a time because of his crazy yoga skills, very few women on the planet would actually want to have sex for that long. It would get boring after a while, and in the worst case, it would start to hurt.

I do have a point here besides making you all feel better about your-selves. Having sexual hang-ups like these will only put undue stress on your life, and ultimately, they tend to be self-reinforcing and reifying. The easiest way to get over these insecurities are more is to get over yourself. If you take yourself too seriously—especially what people do in bed, which is from a detached perspective, anyway, quite comical—sex will always suck for you, and not in the good sense of "suck" as it normally pertains to sex. Sex should be fun, not terrifying. If, however, you have *really, really bad sexual anxiety* (technically named "RRBSA"[16] in the DSM-IV), it may be helpful to see a therapist. This is *especially* the case if your anxiety stems from past sexual abuse. In this case, I cannot recommend strongly enough that you seek therapy, as such abuse can express itself in destructive and dangerous behavior, sexual and otherwise.

---

penises on average than the rest of us. I have no idea why, although I suspect it probably has something to do with the whole World War II thing. Don't worry, however, if you're German. Condomi—as far as I know—now makes slightly smaller condoms for your slightly smaller junk. Or at least, they had plans to some years back. And no, I did not make any of this up. Seriously.

16 This I did make up. Seriously. But you should still see a therapist if you think your anxiety is more serious than "the norm," whatever that is, precisely.

Signs things are just not going to work

1. They tell you to "go to hell" at least once a day.
2. They try to embarrass or humiliate you publicly.
3. They slip animal products into your food.
4. They hit you in a non-friendly, non-joking kind of way.
5. They prey upon your fears and insecurities, like the shrewd vultures they are.
6. They get along with your family (unless that's a good sign for you).
7. They know you read this.
8. They use readily use PCs over Apple computers, or Linux boxes.
9. You are dating any of my exes.

Fucking Ethically

While blowjobs are vegan, there are still a number of ethical concerns as they pertain to sex, and in particular, vegan sex, beyond if your lubes and gear are cruelty-free. In particular, I'm talking about sadism, masochism, and abortion. BDSM[17] is probably a bit less complicated than the whole abortion debate, so if you'll indulge me, I'll tackle that one first.

I'm a firm believer that what you choose to do in the bedroom is your business and yours alone. I'm also a firm believer that a little light B&D can be fun. I am not a firm believer in S&M, though, and I'll tell you why, with no expectation that it will stop you from engaging in it if that's your thing, and with no judgments about you personally. The sexualization of violence is a potentially dangerous slippery slope, and frequently—but not always—involves the objectification of the person on the receiving end. It is my perspective that this is not in line with the ethics of veganism, which abhor the objectification of other beings, as well as unnecessary violence. I'm not saying you're a bad person or

---

17 BDSM = Bondage/Discipline, Domination/Submission, Sadism/Masochism

not vegan if you are into S&M; rather, I'm merely suggesting you question exactly *why* you are into S&M. But like I said, what you do behind closed doors is your own business.

Abortion is a little trickier. Well, actually, I don't think it's trickier, but some people do. There are what is in my view a surprising number of vegans who are anti-choice. Their position, to the best of my ability to articulate a position diametrically opposed to mine, is that, to quote Mr. Show, "All life is precious, and God, and the Bible." Okay, for some of them. For others, they simply believe that a fetus is a form of life, and like other animals, it's wrong to kill it. For some, abortion is ethically incompatible with veganism.

Here's why I think that's bullshit.[18] While others, most notably Gary Francione (See his book *Introduction to Animal Rights*), have argued this far more eloquently than I am capable of, let me state outright that a fetus, especially in its early stages of development, is wholly different from other "defenseless animals." First of all, fetuses are unique in that they live *inside of* another human being. Second of all, there is no empirical evidence to suggest fetuses within the first trimester, at least, are sentient, possessing the ability to suffer or feel pain—unlike, say, the Bush administration. Therefore, a zygote or a fetus has no inherent interest in continued existence in the way any other animal, human or otherwise, does—but again, unlike the Bush administration. And, since it is incapable of suffering, it has no inherent interest in not suffering any more than does a rock or a blade of grass. In this light, abortion is not in conflict, in any manner, with the ethics of veganism.

Late term abortion, though much rarer, may present a more real ethical conflict. However, the fact remains that the fetus is sustained only by the mother and not viable outside of the womb. While I would like to think the vast majority of late term abortions occur out of a significantly more dire necessity than early term abortions, I don't have any figures in front of me to work from, and I'm not sure such statistics exist. Regardless, as the fetus by itself is not a viable form of life, the

---

18 To put it politely.

termination of a late term pregnancy does not, as I see it, present any major ethical dilemmas so far as veganism is concerned.

Finally, while there are those who will and do articulate religious or quasi-religious arguments about the sacredness of the fetus, I think it grossly unfair to invade on a woman's right to choose based on one's own superstitions.

History

Sexual history is a tricky, sticky topic. After all, there's probably only so much you really *want* to know about your partner's sexual past, and chances are this feeling is mutual. Nonetheless, it can be beneficial, under the right circumstances, to have at least a brief, open, and frank discussion about each other's sexual histories, just so there are no unpleasant surprises later on. What the exact parameters of the discussion are, exactly, is entirely up to the two of you. For instance, you probably *don't* want to hear about what the other person's favorite positions in bed were with their last partner, but you probably *do* want to know about negative past experiences—we nearly all have them, I imagine—and not so you can feel better about yourself, but so you can be more sensitive to things that might trigger less-than-pleasant memories. Of course there are other things to share, not all negative, but the bigger point is that by sharing this information you'll gain a better understanding of, as well as grow closer to, one another.

In sharing these histories, there are some things you'll want to avoid. Don't compare your partner to those of the past. Contrast if necessary, but if you do this too much it will come off the wrong way. At worst, it can make them feel like a rebound. Also, if your partner is clearly becoming uncomfortable with the direction of the conversation, change it. Most importantly, try not to compare yourself to their past partners. Don't ask questions about how you measure up, literally or figuratively, to other people they have been with. This is at least a little tasteless, and really, what point does it serve? Chances are, pretty much everything about you is better than their last partner, otherwise they would still be with them and not you.

Communication

By far the most important thing when it comes to sex—aside from playing it safe—is communication. This can take a variety of forms, both verbal and nonverbal, some of which comes with time as you get to know your partner better. From the outset, it's good to discuss likes and dislikes in a frank but polite way. Guys, if they're using their teeth a little too much during oral sex, it's okay to let them know. Girls, if they're rubbing your clit sore, it's okay to let them know too. Girls and guys, when your partner communicates dislikes to you, don't take it personally. Cheerfully acknowledge what they've said, and simply modify technique or whatever else accordingly. Nothing is a bigger downer than someone who takes sex, or themselves, way too seriously.

Nonverbal stuff is easier to get across. For some people, actually talking about sex can be remarkably difficult. However, no one is a mind reader, and if you don't communicate what you like or don't like, you're only doing yourself a disservice. It's okay to issue critiques and suggestions, just do so gently. It can take time to get things right. Just because you don't click immediately when it comes to sex, doesn't mean things are destined to not work between you and your partner.

Women in particular seem to have a hard time communicating about any and all things sexual. I don't mean this as a harsh criticism; really, it's not their fault. Most of this is a direct result of the way women are raised—well, shiksas anyway[19]—to simply be quiet, accommodating, not rock the boat, don't make trouble, and please their man[20]. Women are raised to think that what they think, the way they feel, ultimately doesn't really matter. At least, not compared to what men

---

19 For some reason, Jewish women may be an exception here. Naomi Wolf, in an interview with *Heeb* magazine, suggests that historically, Jewish women just take less shit and are more open with how they feel than are their gentile counterparts. While I dated my only Jewess when we were in fifth grade, I can say she was, and has remained true to Wolf's characterization her entire life. Then again, I have no idea how this plays out sexually. Like I said, we were in fifth grade. That's a little young, don't you think?

20 Basically, bourgeois WASP values.

think and feel. This kind of social conditioning can be remarkably difficult to overcome. Like so many other things, the only way to get over it is to, well, get over it. This may take plenty of time and practice, but be patient with yourself. Remember, what you have to say is valuable, and equally valid to anything "the boys" might. So don't short change yourself. And men, if you're reading this, it's your job to be sensitive to these things.

My solution to bridging the great sexual communication divide, where it needs bridging, is a bit unconventional, so bear with me. For many couples, communication problems with sex can be really, really difficult to overcome. But I think the best way to do it is that art as old as sex itself: phone sex. Okay, you got me, phones aren't as old as sex itself. But dirty talk, the real essence of phone sex, very well might be. Whether it was the naughty grunts of the first cave men and women, or those special 1-900 phone numbers[21] you tried dialing from pay phones at your local gas station as a kid, talking a little foul can go a long way in helping foster feelings of comfort when it comes to issues of broader sexual communication.

The first place to try this is in bed. If you're one of those people that is really quiet during sex, or just breathes heavily, here's your big chance. Just start being vocal. It'll come to you.[22] You don't have to be a Harlequin novel at first. Hell, the first time around, don't even aim for Penthouse Forum. Just try to squeeze in a few "Oh Gods," or "Oh fucks," or "Oh yeahs," or something (obviously they aren't plural when you say them; if you say them in plural form, you're partner will either think you're polytheistic or have some kind of an unusual lisp). Once you've got that down, try escalating things notch by notch. Next, try being vocal about specific things your partner is doing that you like. How about a breathy, "Oh God, I love it when you _____ my _____,"

---

21 For our international readers, in the U.S., phone numbers that you have to pay to call—you know, beyond your regular phone bill or long distance charges—begin with a 900 prefix. The joke's probably not as funny now that I had to explain it to you, but then it wasn't that funny to begin with.

22 No pun intended.

or something to that effect.[23] From here on out, keep working at it, and things will naturally start to get a little dirtier (read: sexually open) until it's a veritable mudslide of unstoppable sexual commentary, innuendo, and foul, nasty, hotness.

If this doesn't quite work for you, then I should say now that I was one hundred percent serious about the phone sex thing. Now I'm not saying you should dig out some spooge-covered porno mag from the dumpster behind Dunkin' Donuts and call some of the numbers advertised in the back. For one thing, I'm assuming you already have a partner. For another, those cost a lot of money. Also, you really have no way of knowing you're even talking to a member of your preferred gender.

No, put any ideas about those 900 numbers you and your friends tried to call back in middle school straight out of your head. Phone sex is best had with—drumroll—*your partner*. After all, there must be times when they're away or out of town, and you're at home alone, lonely, and horny. It's times such as this that phone sex is a great idea. Of course, if your partner never goes anywhere, this could prove difficult. But if you have cell phones, just go to different rooms in your place and call each other. It's a bit drastic, but it'll do in a pinch. Or, you can ditch the phones entirely, and just jerk off back-to-back. The point is, phone sex *forces* you and your partner to communicate in pretty frank and explicit ways about sexual things, and the benefits extend beyond the immediate one of getting off.

The act of initiating phone sex can be difficult for some people, so I suggest simple but direct statements such as, "I'm not wearing any pants," or, "I'm in bed, and I'm not wearing any pants." or "So, what are you wearing? I'm not wearing any pants." From there, you're on your own, but remember: I have the utmost faith in you, dear reader, and your ability to get off with nothing more than your phone, your dominant hand, and the sweet sound of your partner's voice.

---

23 Quick tip: avoid any dirty talk with words like "Daddy," "Momma," or "Archbishop."

Some Conclusions for the Sex Chapter

Having a healthy sex life is important for any relationship. Well, at least the type of relationship we're talking about in this book. It's neither an important nor healthy part of relationships with parents, pets, or the TV repair guy. But I think you understand what I'm talking about. Anyway, remember to stay safe and communicate. If you can do these two things, the rest of sex will be much easier, less awkward, and more fun. And after all, that's what it's all about, right? Sharing a deeply intimate, but also *fun* experience with the person you love most in the world. It's okay to have some insecurities, or even to be riddled with them. Just don't take yourself so seriously. As with all walks of life, this can get you a long, long way. And if you're ever in doubt of yourself, just dust off that Tom Jones, and dance around in your underwear to "Sex Bomb." Trust me, you'll feel a whole lot better afterwards. So what are you doing still reading this? Go have yourself some hot, ethical, sweet vegan sex. Or if you're still single, go "pleasure yourself" (what a weird expression). Don't worry; I won't tell anyone about the Tom Jones.

chapter 6

The Last Chapter

This chapter was originally titled "Conclusion," but later this struck me as boring. I admit "The Last Chapter" isn't much better, but hey, what would you have called it? You know what, I don't care. Because you didn't write this, I did. By which I mean, my ghost writer. By which I mean, Rush Limbaugh's ghost writer. Okay, so I made that last part up. Also, it's not really as long as a "chapter" should be. So maybe it is more of a conclusion. Ah, fuck.

Actually, "Ah, fuck," sums up my feelings as I finish pounding out this whole sad megillah. I honestly have no idea if this book was any good. I'm of the mind that, regardless of whether or not it gave you some Q.T. with the shitter, it probably wasn't very useful. Frankly, I don't think any relationship advice-oriented books are. That's because they're all bullshit. Most of the "advice" out there sucks, and even if it were useful, it's unlikely you'd follow it anyway. At best, you'll fuck up and do the opposite of what I suggest in these pages, and later chastise yourself thinking, "Damn, I really should have done what that book said. What was it called again? Eh, whatever." Notice how I waited until the *last* chapter to say all this? That's because even if you thought this book totally blows, I still wanted you to spend your hard-earned eleven dollars and some odd change on it.

You're probably wondering what even qualifies me to write a book like this. In all honesty, *jack shit*. But I'm okay with that. No, I'm *more* than okay with that. Because the bulk of relationship advice authors out there don't know what they're talking about any more than me. I guess if anything qualifies me at all, it's that I was the loser-ass no-girl-friend kid growing up who had tons of friends of the opposite sex, all of whom came to me for love advice despite the fact they'd never date me. After every session, they'd make a big point of telling me what a good friend/listener I was, which basically translated to, "You'd be the perfect boyfriend, but you're not popular enough. Sorry." Also, they'd never actually follow my advice, and would later own up to the fact that what I suggested would have been a whole lot more helpful than what they actually did to solve whatever the problem of the day was. Would they follow my advice next time? No. But the point is, I was the one they all came to.

There's a very good chance that you, dear reader, are one of these girls (if you're a girl). Not the exact same ones, of course, but someone just like it; someone who would have asked me for advice in middle school or high school, but would have never actually given me the time of day aside from that, let alone consider going on a date with me. I guess I'm not really bitter about this, just kind of annoyed. But, my publishers tell me I'm going to make something like a dollar per copy sold of this destined-to-be-a-bathroom-reader bad boy, so I suppose we're square now. You've still got my dignity, but at least I have your dollar.

The best I can offer you in all your relationship trials, tribulations, and troubles, is that things work out eventually. I know this because they worked out for me. I'm not saying there's some sort of causal relationship between what works out for me and what works out for you, just that if things work out for even *me*, they'll definitely work out for you. You just have to give it time. You didn't want to read that last sentence, did you? Yeah. Time sucks. Time is against you. Time wants you to die alone, hanging in a closet by the silk-alternative tie you used to autoerotically asphyxiate yourself, lemon wedge stuffed in your mouth, after getting all pilled up. What I mean is, time is bad for you, at least in the beginning.

You've got to turn it around, and make time your lover, your friend, the thing that wants you to successfully choke yourself while you "choke" yourself in the closet with the tie but *without* dying. Or just wank off a lot. Whatever. Point being, while you're on your search, you've got to look at the chaos that is your life as more of a plethora of opportunities. It sounds lame, I know. But it worked for me. And remember, what works for me will totally work for you, because I am the lowest common denominator. You probably thought that was you, but you'd be wrong. Because it's not. It's me. I am the LCD. Getting my point yet?

I guess my point is, I hope this book helps.

Ultimately, I'm doubtless there are many questions I've left unanswered. How about being vegan and having kids? What if such-and-such a thing I said doesn't really work? Chances are, I either can't help you quite yet (kids), or you've got to be a little creative and adaptive (some of the stuff not working). Or, you can write to me for advice through the form at veganfreak.com, or at veganadvice@veganfreak.com. I'll do what I can, and maybe the very thing you need advice on will make it into a future edition of the book. You know, if the first edition actually sells. That, however, remains to be seen.

In a lot of ways, this book is love advice for people who happen to be vegan, and a lot of the stuff probably applies to just about everyone else who isn't. But don't you think it's about time there's a book just for you? I do. I also think it's about time I can afford to pay rent, so make sure to recommend it to people if you it helped[1], or even if you just had a good time spending the two hours it took to read this while you were on the toilet.

In the end, after all the advice and suggestions, all I can really offer you is a friendly "good luck." Oh, and my derision. I've got plenty of that too.

---

1 I was going to edit this, but I figured letting Dan sound like Yoda might be good revenge. You know, he was a total fucking diva about this whole manuscript. Plus, I thought Dan might be upset to have a chapter without footnotes. —ed.

Lightning Source UK Ltd.
Milton Keynes UK
UKHW01f1856140618
324264UK00001B/61/P